SPANISH BAROQUE ART

By SACHEVERELL SITWELL

SOUTHERN BAROQUE ART
A study of Painting, Architecture, and Music
in Italy and Spain of the 17th and 18th centuries,
with 16 illustrations

GERMAN BAROQUE ART
with 49 plates

THE GOTHICK NORTH
with 17 illustrations

VOL. I.   THE VISIT OF THE GYPSIES
VOL. II.   THESE SAD RUINS
VOL. III.   THE FAIR-HAIRED VICTORY

BECKFORD AND BECKFORDISM

BAROQUE ART OF THE KINGDOM OF NAPLES (in preparation)

Photo: August L. Mayes

VALENCIA : PALACIO OF THE MARQUÉS DE DOS AGUAS

Frontispiece

SPANISH BAROQUE ART

*with buildings in Portugal, Mexico, and
other Colonies*

by

SACHEVERELL SITWELL

Author of
" Southern Baroque Art," " German Baroque Art,"
etc.

DUCKWORTH
3 Henrietta Street, W.C. 2
1931

Made *and* printed *in* Great Britain
By The Camelot Press Ltd
London *and* Southampton

CONTENTS

ILLUSTRATIONS

The medallion on the cover is from a gold coin of João V
of Portugal (1706–1750).

TO
GERALD

THE author's thanks are due to Mr. E. A. Cleugh, of H.B.M.'s Consulate-General, Mexico City, and, more especially, to Mr. H. N. W. Bird, of the British Consulate, Oporto, for valuable assistance in securing illustrations for this book. The photographs of buildings in Mexico were supplied by the firm of Hugo Brehme, Mexico City.

PREFACE

THIS book on Spanish Baroque Art has taken a long time to prepare and a still longer time to illustrate. Even now, it is only offered to the public with a good deal of misgiving on the part of the author. It is intended more for a work of information than as a piece of criticism, and this cannot make it easy to read, for it is, of necessity, a catalogue of names and places.

That part of it which deals actually with Spain has been the least difficulty. Spanish Baroque Art produced one masterpiece, the west front of the Cathedral of Santiago da Compostella, known as " El Obradoiro " ; but, apart from that, it presents an extraordinary profusion of small and charming things. These cannot be ignored, because they produce half the colour of the country, and, without them, the sombre landscape would prevail. But they need not be thought of too seriously, for they were not intended for that. They are gay and brilliant, like Spanish tunes ; yet, when that is said, it amounts to a good deal.

Portugal is a very different matter. In this part of the book the author can only hope that a few people may hear, for the first time, of some of the most delightful buildings it is possible to imagine. The northern region, round Braga, is one of the best centres for Baroque architecture in Europe ; and as well as that, all over Portugal there are the azulejos. They form a world of architecture of their own, made of china. It is strange, indeed, that no book has yet been published, in any language, dealing with that strange and extraordinary development of simple tile-work.

It is hoped that the age of João V will appear out of these pages as a pendant to the Manoeline period. It was the second great epoch of Portugal. Recent investigation has made it possible to draw up a nearly complete inventory of the effects it left upon architecture. Some small country towns — Portalegre, Viana do Castelo, Penafiel, Amarante, Lamego, Vila Real — are places unique of their kind, and the fact that they have practically escaped attention until now shows them to us with their architectural beauties untarnished and unspoilt. Practically no one has been to them. They are virgin soil.

After Portugal comes Mexico, with its nine thousand churches of architectural merit. It is obviously impossible to describe even the hundredth part of these, and so a very few selected examples have been chosen out. The interest has been narrowed down, at the end, into the two extraordinary productions of a Creole architect of undoubted genius, after which four more churches representing the most extreme developments of the native Mexican style are examined.

Finally, in order to show the universal spread of the Baroque movement over an area so many times greater than that covered by the Gothic style, some particulars are given of the Jesuit Missions in Paraguay ; of the Portuguese towns of Goa in India and Macao in China ; of an isolated activity of the same ubiquitous race in Abyssinia ; and the book closes with some account of the palaces built for the Chinese Emperors by the Jesuits.

It has, most unfortunately, proved impossible to give anything but the most meagre description of buildings in South America. They exist, in plenty, in Peru and

Ecuador ; in fact, there is not a single State in South America that has not got fine remains of our period. Brazil, in particular ; but no one in Brazil seems to have the very slightest interest in these things. There is an absolute lack of information, and so, for the moment, this part of the project must be allowed to lapse.

By next year it is hoped that a book on the Baroque architecture of the old Kingdom of Naples will be ready. It will account for Southern Italy and Sicily. The splendid buildings in Malta will be added to it. If, one day, a previous book on German Baroque can be revised, and a few pages be added to it dealing with Poland, and more especially with the buildings at Vilna, then an ambitious scheme will have been nearly completed. It will only need a further book, for which there is abundant material, on Northern Italy ; on Rome and Venice and Turin. That will finish the original plan ; and then it will be time to move on somewhere else.

SACHEVERELL SITWELL.

WESTON,
    16th January, 1931.

I

SPAIN

LOVERS of architecture must prefer Spain to Italy. It is a
different problem, altogether, where painting is concerned, but, with architecture, there can be no question
of doubt ; the Spaniards have been the greatest builders
since the Romans. It is our hope, indeed, to prove that
of all the races of Europe the Spaniards, alone, left any
buildings worthy of the name in the new lands they
colonised across the ocean.

But the Spaniards were late in developing their own
idiom. Most of the strictly mediæval work in Spain is
not Spanish in the very least. Except in Catalonia, their
national style did not really appear till the discovery of
America in the reign of Ferdinand and Isabella. Then it
took that hybrid form known as the Plateresque.
Salamanca is, perhaps, the best place in which to study
this ; and other good examples of it are the Church of
San Gregorio at Valladolid and the Hospital of Santa
Cruz at Toledo. Behind all this slightly dubious
exuberance lies the solid achievement of the Spanish
cathedrals, and it is certainly no use trying to find Italian
comparisons for Leon, Burgos, Toledo, Santiago. Nor,
for the matter of that, have the Plateresque buildings any
rivals in other countries. They were the extraordinary
works of an extraordinary people ; for these were the
men who would advance in a handful, almost in a ship's
company, into the middle of populous Indian empires.

The Escurial seems to be antithesis to all this. It is

cold and sombre. It is the personally directed work of
Philip II. Not only does his Austrian Hapsburg blood
show itself in the whole disposition of the place, but, also,
there are the traces in it of his admiration of ancient Rome.
He visited the chief Roman sites in Spain, especially
Merida, and there is no doubt that he was trying to
achieve Roman effects of permanence and endurance in
the Escurial.

After his reign there was a century of poverty. The
Spaniards had overreached themselves. There are but
few buildings of the seventeenth century in Spain, but,
towards the end of that time, a new style evolved itself,
and it is this which forms the subject of these pages. It
was indigenous to the soil of Spain, and it spread from
there to Latin America, more especially to Mexico, where
there was more money, and where, perhaps, it found its
climax.

A new dynasty of kings had come in. They were
French Bourbons, and even the notorious quickness of
Royal families in assimilating themselves to their subjects
could not turn them, at once, into Spaniards. The first
true Spaniard of the race was Charles III (1759–1788).

The buildings to be described are the work of about a
century, from 1680 down till about 1780, or as late as
1790 in the distant countries where tides of taste arrived
later and the old method lingered on long after it was dead
at home. As it was essentially a Spanish movement, the
products of Frenchmen or Italians have entered but little
into the discussion. The Palace of La Granja has not
been described, for it was the work of about three
generations of French sculptors and garden-architects.
Nor does the Royal Palace at Madrid come into mention,
for it was an adaptation by an Italian, Sacchetti, of

Bernini's rejected design for the Louvre. Silence has been preserved, for the same reason, upon the subject of Tiepolo's frescoes in the palace, for, beautiful as they are, their style is necessarily, and markedly, Venetian.

It is to be hoped that in place of these omissions a few new names and a few new places may emerge to show a fresh facet of the Spanish genius. It is not claimed for such things that they are supreme masterpieces in any sense of the word, but their gaiety and ingenuity have given the country much of its colour, and certainly, without them, the sombre landscape would prevail.

The style would seem to have started where, perhaps, it was most needed – in the central tableland of Spain. By fortuitous chance, if not quite undeserved, it is associated for ever with the name of a person who had not really a very great deal to do with it. But since all its vagaries, and particularly those in Mexico, are termed Churriguerresque, it is more simple, here and now, to give some attention to Churriguerra.

We shall find, when we study this architect's work, that he was neither a great master nor a sensationally extravagant designer. Indeed, he was one of the safest and quietest of his contemporaries. He had one peculiar excellence, and that lay in polychrome decoration. It will be described later on, and meanwhile we come back to this problem of why his name has become the synonym for all Spanish extravagances.

The answer appears to lie in his name itself. The sound of the word Churriguerra, if it suggests anything at all, calls to mind a sort of fluttering of edges. Broken and multiple cornices vibrate and glitter together in that word, and anybody who stands for a moment in one of the extreme instances of the style, the Sacristy of the

Cartuja at Granada, will know the accuracy of this architect's name as a word-picture of effects in which he was
not the least important participant.

A great mass of such buildings was produced all over
Spain, and it must be surmised that later and more
" correct " taste hit upon a jumble of names of forgotten
architects, and, by instinct, chose out Churriguerra as the
ringleader. By the end of the eighteenth century these
doctrines were established, and henceforth he has been
held responsible.

José Churriguerra (1650–1723) was a native of
Salamanca, and, in his birthplace, he supervised the
decoration of the Catedral Nueva, remodelled its tower –
a masterly piece of work – and designed the town hall,
or Ayuntamiento. He probably gave sketches, as well,
for the four-storied buildings of the Plaz-Mayor in which
it stands, and this is the finest square of the kind in Spain.
Everybody admires it till they find it is the work of
Churriguerra. The Ayuntamiento is decidedly a beautiful thing, and it is even in fairly correct classical style.
There is nothing to be frightened of here.[1]

Other things by him are some quiet church façades in
Madrid – San Cajetano, for instance – and one or two
portals of palaces. Besides this, some twenty miles from
the city, he designed for Don Juan de Goyeneche the
small palace, the glass-factory, and the entire village of
Nuevo Bastan. It has six streets, four squares, a town
hall, and a prison. Beyond this, but little is known of
Churriguerra. His sons, Geronimo and Nicolo, are
always confused with him, and they completed many of
his works, altering them slightly, no doubt, as they did so.

---

[1] It is strictly of its class ; being no better, nor worse, than the University building
at Valladolid.

The only particular in which this architect calls for trouble is in his system of polychrome decoration. This occurs in the Catedral Nueva. Bright gold, and metallic colours of red and green, are applied as if by some process of lacquer, and they give a delightfully gay effect. This process is important because, in Mexico, it reached to the most extraordinary lengths, as if in emulation of the Indian tapestries made from the wings of humming-birds. A still finer example of this than at Salamanca is in the Chapel of Santa Tecla in Burgos Cathedral. From its appearance it would be impossible to deny it as the work of Churriguerra. It is often ascribed to him, but the point is apparently doubtful, and all that can be said is that, whether by him or not, it represents that architect at his best.[1]

As soon as we leave him on one side and go on to the consideration of other things, we find it all the easier to look back and determine what share of responsibility is really his. There are several buildings in Madrid generally put down to him, but having, in reality, no connection with him. Needless to say, they are more characteristic of the Churriguerresque than anything we have yet come across in dealing directly with his personal achievement. These are the Hospicio Provincial and the Puente de Toledo. Both are by Pedro de Ribera.

This is the man who really deserves Churriguerra's name. He worked a good deal in Madrid, making quiet doorways and portals for the palaces of such families as Miraflores, Torre Hermosa, Montellano, and Arcos. He, also, built a great palace for the Duke of Alba,

---

[1] Churriguerra seems, also, to have specialised in the great formal catafalques of the time, in the manner of Padre Pozzo and the Bibbiena family, e.g. Don Juan de Vera Tassis y Villaroel : *Noticias de la enfermedad de Donna Maria Luisa de Borbon* (Madrid, 1690). This has a plate of the Queen's catafalque designed by Churriguerra and engraved by Ruiz de la Iglesia.

BA

certain, now, to be deserted, in that wild district known as the Batuecos ; and the Ermitage of the Virgen del Puerto, on the Manzanares, which is said to be one of his most successful and ingenious works. He, also, designed the curious barracks at Granada, to be described later on.

As for the Hospicio Provincial and the Puente de Toledo, they are fair instances of excess. But the façade of the Hospicio was intended, and designed, to be seen under every variety of strong light. It is, therefore, deeply undercut and emphatically shadowed. So are the decorations on the Puente de Toledo, for Pedro de Ribera was the man who was praised and extolled, in poems, for his pillars, faceted like the diamonds of Golconda, from out of which the light came gleaming and darting as though they were the actual pillars of the temple. He enjoyed, as may be expected, a special reputation in his day. The effect of the Puente de Toledo is undeniable. It consists of about twelve bastions, rounded like the towers of forts, and decorated, not with balustrades, but with special ornaments, half-vase, half-obelisk. In the middle are two great stone achievements. They have the appearance of Aztec work. The whole affair is in a beautiful golden stone.

But all this is the weakest and least convincing part of the Churriguerresque, and we can move away from Madrid without any regrets. The true achievements of the style have not yet begun, and Madrid is no place in which to search for them. That city has never had fine churches or palaces ; indeed, it is a disappointment in nearly all things except the Prado.

For the purpose of our enquiry it is best to divide Spain into three districts, since there were as many schools

MADRID : HOSPICIO PROVINCIAL

facing p. 18

of architecture, though all of them, especially that which is mentioned third, have their sub-divisions as well. These districts are Valencia with Murcia, Andalusia and Galicia. Then, in conclusion, we will deal with Portugal, a different country and an altogether different culture. That seems to be the only logical method in which to treat a great outburst of building in an immense and unwieldy peninsula. After this, with the total of our experience, we may be competent to discuss the extraordinary developments of the style in lands settled by the Iberians, for a generic term must be used for the joint efforts of Spain and Portugal.

The separate treatment of each section is justified by the fact that nearly all the architects were local men, who never practised out of their native provinces. Every district, as a result of this,· produced its own developments, so that, with even a slight acquaintance, no one could mistake a photograph of Santiago for some place in Andalusia. The details, the method, the whole application, are different, and a confusion of these four provinces is completely impossible if only the mere alternations of climate, and nothing else, are taken into account. It must also be remembered that there were differences even of language ; Valencian (or Catalan), Galician, and Andalusian being separate tongues ; and there is no barrier like that of language.

Now that these three schools are established, and before they receive the separate treatment that must be accorded them, it will be best to treat altogether, and in one section, all the buildings in the rest of Spain outside these three provinces. There are many isolated pieces of work of varying excellence, but, in no case, save at Salamanca when Churriguerra practised in the town,

is there sufficient of it for its products to be called a
distinct school.

The best of these things can be briefly summarised.
There is nothing in Barcelona, and outside it there is little
enough, except the steps to the cathedral at Gerona and
certain buildings in one or two tiny villages in its neighbourhood, such as Fornells, which had its prosperity some
two hundred years ago. At Manresa there is a fine
Jesuit church and convent on a rock above the town.
This has a good façade. There is, also, the old University at Cervara, near Lerida. It is a sombre, Baroque
building of huge size, in style somewhat like a heavy,
lumbering version of Vanbrugh.

It seems unnecessary to discuss Zarogoza. There is
nothing there that comes within our categories, and in all
Aragon it is difficult enough to find anything, if it is not
the Cartuja of Sariñena, which is a typically romantic
Spanish ruin ; an immense church, vast cloisters, and
huge dependencies, the greater part of which date from
our period. It is about eighty miles from Zaragoza.
After this we move to Burgos, and here there is the
Chapel of Santa Tecla, in the cathedral, which has been
already indicated as one of the best things of the Churriguerresque style in the whole of Spain. This chapel is
often the cause of complaint, but any person who keeps an
open mind cannot fail to be impressed by its daring
colour-schemes. It may well be the only thing of the sort
that many people who visit Spain will come across, and,
as such, it deserves more attention than it generally
receives.

What other things are there in Northern Spain ?
There is a most fascinating Churriguerresque sacristy in
the cathedral at Pamplona ; there is a fine church

façade facing down a street at San Sebastian; and near by there is the Sanctuary of St. Ignatius at Azpeitia, but this is not really within our subject, because it is the work of the Roman architect Fontana. Salamanca has been already discussed; at Valladolid there is little or nothing; and at Toledo there is only the Trasparente in the cathedral, the ingenious, but not at all successful, work of a sculptor, Narciso Tomé. It is a maelstrom of limbs, volutes, winged cherubs' heads, and rays of light. At least one epic poem was written about it,[1] but no one can be impressed by it who has seen Bernini at his best, or works of a similar kind by the brothers Asam in such Bavarian monasteries as Wilhering and Osterhofen. These are the successes of the school, and the Trasparente is its failure. But Narciso Tomé could do better than this, for, with his brother, he designed the splendid façade to the University at Valladolid.

This is all ; and out of whole of it perhaps only the work of Churriguerra at Salamanca and at Burgos is worth any serious attention. So we can leave that little on one side, and continue our enquiry into the three districts where the style really flourished. The first of these three shall be Valencia.

The kingdom of Valencia is the part of Spain that is nearest to Italy, and we should expect to find there some traces, at least, of Italian influence. It is, also, only natural that such Italian craftsmen as found their way to Valencia should come from the western seaboard of Italy that directly faces Spain. They would most likely be Neapolitans, marble-workers from Carrara, or Genoese. Between these two latter temperaments and that of the Valencian there is not much natural contact, but it may

---

[1] Francisco Xavier de Casteñeda: "Il Trasparente" (Toledo, 1732).

be imagined that Neapolitans found it easy enough to accommodate themselves to Valencian conditions of climate and environment. In proof of this we shall see that the finest thing of our date in the town, the portal of the Palace of the Marqués de Dos Aguas, is by the sculptor Vergara, a member of an Italian family of craftsmen settled there for several generations.

The province of Valencia is so fertile, and its soil is so rich, that it has always been one of the most prosperous parts of Spain; indeed, this stretch of coast, and the wine-bearing parts of Andalusia, have been, ever since the century of Charles V and Philip II, the only places where building on any considerable scale was not an extravagance of the Court or a reckless squandering on the part of the cathedral chapter. There was money to spend in Valencia, and the effects of this were natural and not strained, however flaunting their form.

There are many beautiful things of our date in Valencia, but the best of them is this Palace of the Marqués de Dos Aguas. This is one of the monuments of the Spanish eighteenth century, and it is in the style to which we must become accustomed if any pleasure is to be had from the highest expression of gay exuberance there has ever been in architecture. If any one thing is certain, it is that the persons who built the palace enjoyed themselves while doing it. We must remember, while we look at it, that the Huerta of Valencia is nearly an earthly paradise. Even now, the Feria of Valencia is a thing without parallel, and wonderful floral games, bull-fights, and battles of flowers are held while it lasts. Such buildings as the Dos Aguas Palace were meant to express and interpret this metropolitan gaiety.

This particular palace is, to begin with, of most

peculiar colour, for it varies according to the light and the time of day between various shades of lilac and green ; so much so, that if asked directly what colour it is, no straight answer can be given. It has, also, and there is no denying it, a distinct likeness in texture to almond paste, though this is no criterion against its merits, for the Doges' Palace looks nicely edible, and so do many other marble buildings in a good light.

The façade of the palace is elaborately panelled, and has two floors of the richest windows imaginable, but the great feature of the building is its doorway. The sides of this are sculptured with colossal figures of Atlantes, while the place of the window in the floor above is taken up by a tremendous array of figures and sun-rays framing in a statue of the Virgin. The sculptor was Ignacio Vergara, and he was carrying out in this the designs of a painter, Hipolito Rovira. Its date is 1740–1744.[1]

Another member of this same family, of Italian descent, Francisco Vergara, was the sculptor of the façade of the principal doorway of the cathedral. But it was by a German architect, Konrad Rudolf. It is, indeed, only the rich golden stone of which it is composed that makes this façade Spanish and not typically Bavarian or Austrian. In character it has a particular resemblance to the churches of Fischer von Erlach at Salzburg ; to Fischer von Erlach, that is to say, in the early part of his career. The actual doors of the cathedral are plated with a most beautiful rose-tinted silver, and the whole plan of the thing, with its centrepiece and advanced hemi-cycle wings, makes a delightful interlude to a not otherwise superlatively interesting cathedral.

[1] On two successive visits it has been impossible to obtain entry into the palace, and I have never yet seen any description of the interior. Even if the original decoration of the rooms is destroyed, there should be a fine staircase.

After the palace and the façade of the cathedral the great features of Valencia are its towers and its domes. The best of the towers is that to the Church of Santa Catalina, which is by the architect J. B. Viñas. It is hexagonal, and has five floors of windows, of different design for each story. As for the domes of Valencia, their interest is in the fact that they are tiled, for here we are in the country of azulejos, the invention and use of which date from the time of the Moors. These azulejos are an important part of Spanish decoration, and one which has not yet received sufficient attention or appreciation. Here, in Valencia, the art is of comparatively simple and modest importance, which is not the case in Andalusia. In Mexico, particularly at Puebla, the azulejos are the chief decorative feature ; while, in Portugal, this art reached to an extreme perfection which must be dealt with, at some length, when that country is described.

That is in the future, and in the meantime there is Valencia, half indicated, as yet, as to its late buildings. The most interesting of them, after the Dos Aguas Palace, is the Church of los Santos Juanes. And this serves as introduction to almost the only name in these pages that has not a purely regional importance. This is the painter Antonio Palomino (1653–1725), who is met with, also, at Salamanca and at Granada. He was a most able decorative painter and an extremely learned man, as shown in his *Museo Pictorico*, a history of painting in Spain written after the manner of Vasari and of a comparable importance where Spain is concerned. In the Church of los Santos Juanes the whole vault of the church is painted by him, and it is a performance worthy of an Italian master, of Pietro da Cortona or of Luca Giordano.

The whole church, apart from that, is of extreme interest, and comes down to us quite untouched out of the curious times we are discussing. It is in a quarter of the town that is full of slums and old houses. Nearly everything in sight is in harmony with that date, more especially the huge blue dome of the Escuelas Pias.

The other fine things in Valencia must jostle each other in a single paragraph. These are the Chapel of the Desamporados, which joins on to the cathedral and has another fine painting by Palomino ; and the azulejos in the Churches of San Sebastian, San Andres, and upon the staircase, and in the court, of the Church of the Milagro. These are simple enough ; it is only the beginning of the art.

In the immediate neighbourhood of Valencia there is the Cartuja de Porta-Coeli, with a tiled cloister and refectory. They are the latest work in a wonderful old abbey. In its time it was the third most important monastery in Spain, but now it is deserted, and is hardly visited even by the few people living in Valencia who are interested in such things. Nevertheless, it is easily accessible, being only some twenty miles from Valencia, and it is one of the most beautiful of all the old Spanish abbeys.

The only other town in this district that we need mention is Villareal de la Plana, a most delightful place in the middle of vast orange-groves. The tiled cupolas, the palm-trees, the water-pitchers of classical shape carried on the women's heads, the omnipresent smell of the orange-groves – all these things people, as it were, the Baroque architecture of this little town, and make it one of the most delightful spots imaginable. There are several churches ; but the best of them is the cathedral, of imposing size, and with a most admirable octagonal tower in brick. Altogether, no one who visits Villareal de la Plana will regret it. The Southern atmosphere and the capricious shapes of the buildings are a perpetual inspiration. There is a great deal of good tile-work here; but close to it is the little town of Alcora, where the tiles were actually made, and the Ermita de los Dolores is as fine a piece of this decoration as can be seen in the province of Valencia.

To conclude this account, a little space must be devoted to the island of Majorca, for in Palma, the capital, there was considerable activity in building, down to a late period. This is especially seen in the palaces, many of which have fine, bold staircases rising out of their courtyards. Such are the Vivot, d'Ayamans, and Sollerich palaces. Some of them have delightful interiors frescoed by local painters. As well as these, there is a magnificent Churriguerresque doorway to a chapel in the cathedral, and doorways, obviously by the same hand, decorate the façade of S. Francisco and the Church of Monte Sion. The sculptor's name was Pedro Orrach.

We must now go south from Valencia into the kingdom of Murcia, and we are in the region where something interesting may spring up in even the smallest village, up to the frontiers of Granada. It is about the pleasantest part of Spain. There were no great architects, but they could create beauty with a few simple lines. The sculpture is always good, and, where trouble had to be taken – a retablo or a doorway – they spared no pains, and the results are often of a dazzling intricacy.

The towns of Gandia and Jatiba are typical of such places. The first of these has the imposing palace of the Borja family. It has a fine staircase and magnificent

MURCIA : FAÇADE OF THE CATHEDRAL

state-rooms, with stucchi and frescoes by Gaspar de la Huerta. But the town of Orihuela is better than either of these. This small place is literally full of beauties, and there is at least one immense church, S. Domingo, with a monastery at the back of it, that has two double cloisters and a refectory lined with azulejos.

The four seaboard towns, Alicante, Cartagena, Almeria, and Malaga, are all disappointing in this respect. There is practically nothing in them. The villages and small market-towns in their neighbourhood, on the other hand, have nearly all of them got churches and palaces of our date. But we cannot delay over them; we must get to Murcia.

This is a most exquisite town, and the smaller delicacies of Baroque art can be studied here as nowhere else. The churches and convents are numberless, and so are the tiled domes of blue and green. But, first of all, there is the façade of the cathedral, one of the best Baroque façades in Europe. It is generally ascribed to Jaime Bort, but apparently he only carried out the plans of a military engineer, Sebastian Feringant y Cortes. This man is said to have been of French origin, but nothing more seems to be known about him except that he directed the arsenal at Cartagena. The façade, which is of a lovely golden stone, is like a piece of cabinet-work carried into an immense scale. There has never been such a play of broken pediments, or so successful a use of statues to people a façade and keep all its details in position.

He seems not to have touched the interior, but merely added this frontispiece to it. Nor are any of the smaller things in Murcia designed by him ; they are the works of various local architects, whose names, were they given here, would only encumber the text. But there is one other name associated with Murcia, and that is the sculptor Francisco Zarcillo, the last of the great poly-chrome sculptors of Spain, and, himself, of Neapolitan origin. He is the last of a long line, Berruguete, Becerra, Martinez Montañes, Pedro de Mena, Alonso Cano ; but none of these sculptors were so lucky with their settings as Zarcillo. Nearly every one of the tiled domes of Murcia covers some statue by him. The *pasos* – groups to be carried in procession during Holy Week – are in the round Ermita de Jesus. The Churches of San Juan, San Miguel, Santo Domingo, and Santa Eulalia, have statues by him, and so has the magnificent Baroque monastery of San Jeronimo, outside the town. Also, in fairness to Cartagena, it must be said that the Church of Santa Maria de Gracia, in that town, has some fine things by him. Murcia is full of them, and, as has been said, there can hardly be another town of its size with so many chapels and little Baroque churches. Nor is there another town in Spain so beautiful to walk in, for, at every step, there is a tiled façade, or a sculptured doorway. Only a hundred years ago Murcia must have been a place of incredible beauty. Imagination and sense of fitness have seldom worked so close together in any town.

This is the end of our first province, and nearly every-thing worthy of attention in either Valencia or Murcia has been mentioned. It is not Andalusia ; the character is entirely different. Valencia, as a big city, is one of the most unspoilt things that have come down to us out of this past of two centuries ago, and it had most certainly an architecture especial to itself. This comes out in all sorts of curious ways, so that no one who knows Valencia will be surprised that Fortuny, the Spanish contemporary and equivalent to our Fred Walker, came from there. His origin seems to be implicit in this now neglected painter's work ; and the case is the same, though one need not mention him, with Sorolla. Both of them are typical Valencians, though how and why this should be so, it is difficult to say.

If we continue straight down from Murcia into Andalusia, towards Granada, we come to the town of Lorca. This is still in Valencia, but it is so near to Andalusia that it must be taken on the way to Granada. Lorca is a town with about eighty thousand inhabitants, but no foreigners ever visit it. In the eighteenth century it was extremely rich, and this prosperity has left many happy marks upon the town. The following churches — the Rosario, San Mateo, San Francisco, Carmen, Ermita de Gracia, San Pedro, Santa Maria, San Juan — are all of our period. That makes eight churches in this one town ; all of them have splendid Churriguerresque work, many have sculptures by Zarcillo, and nearly all of them have paintings by the local artist, Camacho. There is, also, the Collegiale de San Patricio, an immense church with many paintings by Camacho and a Churriguerresque sagrario ; and, in the way of palaces, that of the Guevara family, with a splendid doorway of 1693, a staircase of Herculean size, and windows with admirable ironwork grilles.

Lorca is, in fact, a town of the late seventeenth century, owing nothing whatever to outside influences ; it was a centre of local provincial activity. It was a rich town, with money enough to work out its own peculiar archi-tectural lines, and it would be difficult to think of any better interpretation of this land of heat, with its near prospects of vineyard and orange-grove. It must be

thought of, also, as background for the beautiful local
costumes ; in fact, these buildings are a sort of stage-
work ; they must be seen as a setting for such effects,
and, once they are thought of like that, there can no longer
be any doubt as to the degree of success they have
achieved.

Between Lorca and Granada is the town of Guadix.
We are in Andalusia. Guadix has a good cathedral, with
rich Churriguerresque choir-stalls, but the chief feature
of the town is the Barrio de Santiago, a hillside full of
rock-dwellings which are lived in by the gypsies. It is
like a smaller Albaicin, and it means that Granada is near
by. Already the landscape is like Granada. It is only
green for two months of the year ; the rest of the year it is
bare and brown. The landscape in Morocco is very little
different from this; it might be Fez instead of Granada.

That town has two outstanding works of our period ;
the Cartuja, and the Castillo de Bibataubin. Théophile
Gautier seems to have been the first person to appreciate
the Cartuja. He realised the truth about it, which is that
it was a definite attempt to rival the intricacies of the
Alhambra on the part of one or two persons who had the
leisure and the patience to devote their lives to this one
thing. It is a parallel to the Alhambra, but in another art.

Those parts of the Cartuja with which we are concerned
are the sagrario and the sacristy. The sagrario, which is
of marble, jasper, and porphyry, is by F. Hurtado
Izquierdo, who worked at it from 1704 till 1720, and the
vault above it is frescoed by Palomino. But it is the
sacristy that is important. This represents thirty-seven
years of work, from 1727 to 1764, by Luis de Arevalo.
The cedarwood cabinets inlaid with ivory, mother-of-
pearl, tortoiseshell, ebony, and silver, are thirty-four

GRANADA : SACRISTY OF THE CARTUJA

years' work, from 1730 to 1764, by a Carthusian monk, Fray José Manuel Vasquez. This room represents the lifework of two men ; it is a *tour de force*, an extraordinary and transcendental piece of work that is unlike anything else the eyes have ever seen.

Its snowy whiteness cannot be described, but it is formed out of innumerable close edges, fluttering and never touching, and the eyes can only tell them apart by the thin ledges of shadow between them. The pallor of this intense stucco-work is relieved by pilasters of red marble with white and pink veins, and by the prevailing tortoiseshell in the vestment cupboards and in the door.

The intricacy and richness of the whole effect have arrived at the same degree of perfection as in the best Moorish work – the honeycomb vaults of the Alhambra, or Tlemcen. The sacristy is a unique thing, and when first seen it delights the eyes as do the filigree courts of the Alhambra. Perhaps if one lived in Granada one would tire of them both, except by moonlight.

The other curiosity of Granada is the Castillo de Bibataubin. This is a piece of military architecture, a barracks ; but, as such, it is outside ordinary human experience. It looks like the work of someone who was intoxicated by military music, by the slow, tapping marches of the time. Also, it appears to be consecrated to the Prussian Guard, who must have been the models of the military system all over Europe at that period of the Seven Years' War. Not only do the walls of the building seem to be plastered with pipe-clay, but, at the corners, there are statues of grenadiers wearing the high, half sugar-loaf hats of the Prussian Guard. Their wigs are powdered and tied down into a pigtail ; they have fierce bristling moustaches, and their muskets are on their

shoulders. There is a big monumental doorway in the
middle of the façade, an affair of luxuriously entwined
pillars, and above these, again guarded by grenadiers,
sits a lion on a cushion, brandishing a drawn sword and
wearing a crown.

The architect of this was Pedro de Ribera, the designer
of the Puente de Toledo at Madrid, and, here again, this
unknown man deserves everything in the way of abuse
that has fallen on the undeserving head of Churriguerra.
It is a beautiful thing, though; and one most eminently
suited to the strange and formal drill that the troops
underwent, and to parade-antics such as the goose-step.
If one laughs at the Castillo de Bibataubin, then one must
laugh at our own Grenadiers slow-stepping to Handel's
slow march from *Scipio*. Certainly Granada is a most
unlikely place in which to find this barracks. It seems to
epitomise so much of eighteenth-century life – its military
uniforms, its military music, its conceptions of war. The
inhabitants of Granada must have thought so, too, particularly any recruits who found themselves lodged there.

These two things, the Cartuja and the barracks, make
a fit supplement to Granada, and bring it down into the
eighteenth century as a centre of things improbable and
unlikely. Nothing is more improbable than that the
palace of the Moorish kings should still be in existence, and this pair of Churriguerresque buildings most
decidedly complete the list of hazards. Unfortunately,
there are no important palaces of our period in Granada,
and, indeed, except for gilding in most of the churches,
there is nothing more for us to delay over.

We now come to Seville, and in the capital of Andalusia there is a great deal of late seventeenth-century work,
but nothing of exceptional merit. Yet the character of

the whole town is a grafting of this period on to principles of house-construction that were Moorish in origin. These essentials were kept to very closely, so that the town has great homogeneity. There is no other town in Europe, save Venice, where every small alley is so typical of the whole city. But a strange lethargy seems to have overtaken Seville early in the seventeenth century, and nothing of any moment seems to have happened since then. It may have come from contentment ; from the feeling that there was enough already of everything they wanted.

In order to complete the cathedral, the sagrario was built on it, and the project was finished about 1670. The exterior is a fine and complicated flight of stone, of true Southern character, rich and exuberant, and it is about the last considerable work done in Seville, if we except the tobacco factory and the Palace of San Telmo. Both these have typical Churriguerresque façades. The strains of *Carmen* seem to pervade the first of them,[1] and the second has an interest of another kind, because it was the palace of the Duc de Montpensier, and the " Laocoön " of El Greco used to hang there.

These few buildings apart, Seville, so far as our date is concerned, is an affair of churches. No single one of these calls for special attention, but among the best of them is that of the Caridad. It is an agreeable Baroque building with five azulejo mosaics, designed by Murillo upon its façade. The interior contains six of Murillo's better paintings and four pictures by a more interesting artist, Valdés Leal of Cordoba[2] (1622–1690). But the real point of this hospital is the purely romantic one that

[1] Cf. the English libretto of *Carmen*. *Chorus :* " Is yonder high building the place where young women are employed at cigarette-making ? " *Don Camillo :* " It is ! "

[2] This artist did the plates for almost the only fine Spanish book of our period; La Torre Farfan : *Fiestas de Sevilla* (1672).

CA

it was founded by Don Miguel de Mañara, whom legend fixed upon as the original of Don Juan de Tenorio. He led an authentic life of vice and debauchery, repented, and obtained admission to his own hospital as *hermano mayor*. His portrait, by Valdés Leal, is shown there, in the dress of the *hermano mayor*, and the sword he wore as a Knight of Calatrava is still to be seen, together with his death-mask.

Owing to the fact that Seville had no architect of any eminence, we must not expect to find much more work of our period. There are, however, two churches – those of the Salvador and of San Luis – that have interesting points about them. Generally speaking, these churches of Seville are disappointing compared with those of Valencia. They have a thousand picturesque and weather-worn effects, but these are mostly the result of age and accident. Even the tiled domes are of inferior colouring, often with a predominant note of coarse blue in them. The churches cannot have been any better when they were new, and this is always a safe criterion in judging the merits of building. Any really fine work should inspire regret that it was not possible to see it in pristine condition, for beauty should come on purpose and not by accident. Seville is a town of whitewashed houses and crumbling churches. In retrospect, it is only the houses that are remembered. Had Charles III carried out his intention of making Seville into the capital of Spain we should have had, here, some of the finest buildings of Europe, but this project was never more than discussed, and Seville, with its unique and extraordinary atmosphere, survives by this and not by its buildings. There is Seville Cathedral, and it is difficult to remember any other churches but that.

Cordoba was more lucky than Seville, but this is
chiefly a matter of the building material. This was a
golden stone, like the stone of Syracuse or Lecce, and it
made fine and dramatic effects. There are, also, some
excellent pictures by the Cordoban painter, Valdés Leal,
in the Church of El Carmen. Besides this, in Cordoba,
we must mention the pulpits in the coro of the cathedral
by a Frenchman, Michel Verdiguier, and the choir-stalls
by Pedro Cornejo. This same Verdiguier designed the
Triunfo de San Rafael, a statue on a pedestal above the
Guadalquivir.

There now remain the three Andalusian towns of
Cadiz, Jerez, and Ronda, after which some of the smaller
towns of Andalusia must be mentioned, because they
often contain more than the big cities. The position with
regard to these three towns can be very briefly stated.
Cadiz has nothing in it to delay us. The cathedral is a
heavy Greco-Roman affair, only interesting because
Haydn wrote music specially for the chapter. There are
no churches of our period, and no palaces.

Jerez has, in the first place, a much more pleasant
character than Cadiz, which is sinister and horrible. It
may be the lunatic asylum, Santa Catilina, with its
Murillos ; or it may be having read in Gautier's travels
of the bull-fight he saw there, when the banderillas had
been dipped in sulphuric acid, but Cadiz is not like Andalusia at all. It is much more mournful, being in a sort of
perpetual moonlight from the violence of its own white
shadows. The eyes correct them into white, but they are
really blue. Jerez, on the other hand, has the golden
stone that is always such an advantage, for it is a beautiful
thing, in itself, apart from the effects wrought into it.
Also, it is still an extremely prosperous place, owing to its

wine trade. Jerez has an abundance of small and charming details, but nothing of any great importance, except the Cartuja, a few miles outside the town. This is a ruin of the most exquisite beauty, with excellent work in all three styles, Gothic, Plateresque, and Baroque. Their harmony is complete, and there is no jarring note between them.

This was, once, the greatest monastery in all Andalusia. It is, now, only a wreck, and even the pictures by Zurbaran that adorned it have been removed, and are either in private collections outside Spain or in the museum at Cadiz. Much space could be given to the cloisters, the chapter hall, and the church ; but the interest of our own period must confine us to the façade of the church, which is a splendid work of 1667. It is in the local, Martellilla stone, of golden hue, and it consists of two stories of eight pillars each. In the centre of the second story there is a huge rose-window framed in by a broken pediment ; and the attic above this consists, again, of two members, the lower with a statue of St. Bruno, and the higher with the doves and emblems of the Holy Ghost. All the carvings of the façade are in the sharpest and most vigorous relief, and the statues are exceptionally fine, which is due to the fact that Alonso Cano worked for some time upon them. Apart from his share in it, the name of the architect is unknown, but the work ranks as one of the most successful additions to an existing atmosphere that has ever been achieved. It is over a century later in date than the church itself, or the Plateresque gate to the monastery, and yet it is in perfect keeping, and seems only to continue something already existing and of ancient growth.

Of the big towns only Ronda now remains, and this

has two fine things in it. The first of these is the bull-
ring, built late in the eighteenth century by the Real
Maestranza, the oldest order of nobles in Andalusia.
It is the classical example of what a bull-ring should be,
comparatively small in size, but of unsurpassable fitness
to its purpose. It has some wrought-iron balconies with
scenes of bull-fights which make a good external show of
the ancient tauromachic traditions of the place, for Ronda
was the centre of one of the two great schools of bull-
fighting. The other fine thing in Ronda is a superb late
seventeenth-century window-grille. It is a sort of
elaborate, metal bird-cage, from behind which the women
could carry on whispered conversations with their
gallants, and this is the transcendental example of such
moonlit convention.

Specimens of Spanish balconies, nearly as good as this
but never quite up to the romantic Rondena standard,
can be seen in many of the little Andalusian towns, more
particularly in San Fernando, which is on the way to
Cadiz. The houses are one-storied and whitewashed, as
though they were summer-pavilions, and nearly all of
them have these "jalousies" outside their windows,
which throw a beautiful shadow, like a cage, upon the
white wall at their side. The air, at San Fernando, is
generally absolutely charged with blue ; it is not only the
sky that does this, but also the sea, which has an un-
believable depth of colour, and flashes as if it were an
electric reflecting mirror put there on purpose to do this.
In the distance, outside the town, there are marshes with
white ibises feeding in them, and white pyramids of salt
standing near together in groups, like an encampment of
giant tents. Here and there are the authentic barracoons,
little forts built by the Spaniards against Moorish pirates.

Altogether, though there is little enough of any special architectural note in it, San Fernando is one of the most romantically beautiful things in Spain, and it has that spotless, white cleanliness which is a feature of all Andalusian villages, and is so different from the small towns in Southern Italy.

Finally, between Seville and Cordoba we must notice the two delightful towns of Carmona and Ecija. Nothing could be imagined that is more charming than Carmona. No streets are cleaner, least of all in England, and the whole town looks as if it was repainted every year. The result of this is an atmosphere that is curiously Dutch, in some particulars. There are several red-brick, late seventeenth-century houses, and this, of course, much assists such very pleasant illusions. These houses are models of brick architecture, and they make an excellent contrast to the all-pervading whitewash of the rest of the town. A walk in Carmona is a revelation, but in what this consists it is difficult to say. It is a town of wonderful results won by little effort.

As to Ecija, no place could be more suitable in which to stress these remarks on late Spanish architecture. It was Théophile Gautier who first noticed this extraordinary town. He felt as if he had arrived in a new country of pagodas and Hindu temples, with strange porcelain statues and monuments. This is an accurate description. There are three church towers faced with azulejos, and several china monuments and fountains. The narrow alleys of the town are of a blinding whiteness. Ecija is the hottest town in Europe, and this is impressed upon the mind at every step. It has palaces as well as churches, and the most delightful thing of all is the palace of the Marqués de Peñaflor. Its picturesque character is indescribable ; the curved façade with its flowered window-boxes ; the Salamonic door, and still more Salamonic staircase ; the interior courtyard. This should have been the palace of Don Juan de Tenorio. Everyone who visits Seville should go to Ecija to see it, and we will conclude these notes on Andalusia, in front of this example of provincial luxury and phantasy. It has as much poetry in it as anything else in Spain.

The most splendid achievement of Spanish Baroque art has been left till last. It is the one instance in which proportions of a really monumental nature were reached, and perhaps the name of the architect is the one really great name to be remembered. It is Fernando Casas y Novoa, and the scene of his labours was Santiago da Compostella. He was a Galician by birth, and was trained by D. A. de Andrade, his predecessor in the office of cathedral architect. The resources at the disposal of the chapter, early in the eighteenth century, must have been enormous, for they undertook at that date the erection of an entirely new west front and the reconstruction of the whole of the interior. Besides this, an ambitious scheme was carried to completion which remodelled the square in front of the cathedral and made it into one of the finest things of its kind in Europe. There is nothing to compare with it except St. Mark's Square in Venice and the Place Stanislas in Nancy.

The western façade of the cathedral, known as El Obradoiro, is among the most magnificent achievements of Baroque art. It was completed in 1738. It consists of an immense body, flanked by two stupendous towers, two hundred and thirty feet high ; and all of this stands on a ramp above a double, external staircase that rises in

two flights, with a double row of balusters. The façade
spreads itself over the base of the towers, and consists of
two stories and a gable. Each story is flanked by a pair
of Corinthian pillars, and, above that, rises the immense
gable, ending in a cupola, and having, first, two niches,
and then one gigantic niche, that hold statues, increasing
in their size, of St. James. On either side of this, spring
the towers, in two diminishing stories, ending in a balustrade of obelisks, and a pair of great buttressed cupolas.
The lower parts of the towers, up to the first story – and
this is at the height of the final statue of St. James, in the
gable – are, as it were, lined with five Doric pilasters on
each of their faces ; and this gives the tower an extraordinary appearance of strength. The celebrated Romanesque Portico de la Gloria is immediately behind El
Obradoiro.

A later architect, who really initiated the Classical re-
vival in Spain, Ventura Rodriguez, designed the façade,
known as the Azabacheria, to the north front of the transept. This, also, is an extremely fine work, in two
stories, with two projecting wings, and a gable.

The interior of the cathedral was much altered in the
eighteenth century. Nearly all the chapels have monuments of our period. The capilla mayor is completely
the work of that time. The high altar is an immense
affair made out of alabaster, jasper, and silver ; and was
designed, about 1715, by Figuera. The actual altar was
made by him from eleven hundred pounds of silver ; and
it shows St. James, seated, with four kneeling kings holding in front of him an image of himself. Above the altar
is a censer, six feet high, called El Botafumeiro, which
is so heavy that it is swung from side to side by a rope, or
an iron chain. This little detail serves to give an idea of

SANTIAGO DA COMPOSTELLA : EL OBRADOIRO

the scale on which the services in the cathedral are still maintained. As many as forty-eight canons are attached to it, and on occasions there is a bag-pipe band.

The other sides of the square in front of the cathedral are taken up by the Hospital Real, built by Enrique de Egas in the time of the " Catholic Kings," and the Palacio Consistorial, built in 1766–1772, a very fine building with an equestrian statue of St. James on its façade. There are many other things in Santiago which are interesting from their architecture. There is yet another façade to the cathedral, opposite the Azabacheria, and in front of it is the Casa del Cabildo, designed, probably, by another good local architect, Simon Rodriguez. It is a small façade with a front of six windows, and an extremely rich roof-line of balustrates and pinnacles, with a little gable framing in a great achievement of a heraldic nature formed from the cockle-shell of St. James.

This same architect, Simon Rodriguez, designed the façade to the Church of San Francisco, a strict, cold, Palladian composition, and the front to the old Cistercian monastery of Monfero, outside the town. This might almost be in Vicenza, for the whole façade of three floors is contained by four vast Corinthian pillars, and the unfinished tower was to have been a round drum walled in with Doric pilasters. But the great invention of Simon Rodriguez was his church for the nuns of Santa Clara, which is one of the most peculiar conceptions in all Baroque architecture. It is of very small dimensions, and the design is reticulated in the heavy, massive, grey stone. It is nearly as impossible to describe as the buildings by Borromini in Rome ; but the top of the façade is like a great rounded hood, topped by an ornament like the section of a pillar reposing on a square block. This is repeated lower down, on either side, above the downward curves of the hood. The heavily barred windows of the convent add to its formidable effect.

Even now, the interest of Santiago is not exhausted, for we have not described the Convent of San Martin Pinario, its immense gilded retablo full of equestrian figures, fighting as though in battle, and its fine choir-stalls ; but all such things are subordinated to that one really wonderful achievement, El Obradoiro, the western façade of the cathedral by Fernando Casas y Novoa. There is nothing so fine as this, of its date, in Spain ; and there is nothing to equal it in Italy. It is the superb culmination to one of the most wonderful cathedrals of the civilised world ; while the little façade to Santa Clara proves that there was a minor local architect, in Santiago, not inferior to Bernini or Borromini in the originality and strength of his ideas. Santiago is in the remotest corner of Spain ; but its architecture is of the kind that should mark the centres of civilisation.

SANTIAGO DA COMPOSTELLA : CONVENT OF SANTA CLARA

II

PORTUGAL

PORTUGAL has both a history and a material past that are out of all proportion to its present importance, or to its size as a country. The monuments of its greatness are in a style of architecture so peculiar that it is without parallel ; the monasteries of Batalha and Tomar have literally to be seen to be believed. They were the products of a golden age, when the inhabitants of this small kingdom found India and Africa and Brazil at their mercy. It was the reign of Emmanuel I (1495–1521).

Then came the decline, the defeat of the young King Sebastian in Morocco, the Spanish dominion, and finally the restoration of independence under the Dukes of Bragança in 1640. In our special province, that of architecture, practically nothing had happened for a century. The full classical renaissance is hardly to be found, save in the Palladian cloister at Tomar, which dates from about 1560. Apart from that, there is a complete break in building activity up till the end of the seventeenth century. This is because, even when it had regained its independence, the country was at the lowest possible ebb of its fortunes, and was only able to maintain itself by making abject and degrading treaties with the Dutch and with the English. But, in spite of this, another time of prosperity was in store for Portugal.

It was the gold and the diamonds of Brazil, and this new wealth glittered, so to speak, over the entire reign of João V (1706–1750). It was an age of fabulous splendour and magnificence in everything that concerned the king and the Church. The rest of the population were in the position of starving spectators at this elaborate show. By no standards whatever can João V be called a great king, and yet, as a spectacle, there has been nothing like it. There has seldom been a human being with so much money to spend, or one so free of all restraints. There is nothing, even in the history of the Romanovs, to compare with it.

The fruits of this luxury were destroyed by two things – by the Lisbon earthquake of 1755, and by the efforts of Pombal, the Minister of João's successor, Joseph I. This last, and designed, destruction may have been good politics, but it destroyed one of the most extraordinary states of affairs that has ever existed in any country, and we must regret it for that reason. In Lisbon, itself, nearly everything perished in that disastrous earthquake. The only things left to us as evidence are the Royal coaches at Belem, the treasure of São Roque, and the Germain collection of silver.

Throughout the rest of the country there is ample material, but, Lisbon and its district apart, there are two distinct regions where building on a big scale was in progress. These are the Algarve and the province of Oporto, and they must be our fields of enquiry ; but, to these things, the King and his own buildings may be taken as prelude, and, even before that, the sources of his wealth must be indicated. It all came from Brazil.

The first consignment of gold to reach Portugal arrived in the year 1699, and the revenue to the Portuguese Crown from the King's fifth part, in spite of much fraud, was estimated at £300,000 a year. Later on, the discovery of diamonds in the newly conquered (1750) Paulist republic further increased the wealth of the King, and, in addition to the Royal right to every diamond of above twenty carats' weight, the King was estimated to make an income of £100,000 a year by a contract entered into with a syndicate of English diamond-buyers.

Further details may be given in order to emphasise this sudden flow of riches. In 1711, out of an annual revenue of 25,000,000 of French francs, the colonies only contributed 1,800,000 ; but, by the middle of the century, Brazil, alone, gave a revenue of 32,000,000 francs. The only persons to benefit were the Royal family and the Church. The country was in abject poverty.

The King must have spent vast sums upon the palace at Mafra. It is the biggest relic of his reign. The plan was drawn up by a German architect, J. F. Ludwig, of Ratisbon, after sketches by the great Juvara had been rejected. The foundation stone was laid on 17th November, 1717, this ceremony alone costing upwards of £40,000. As a rule, 14,700 workmen were employed, but when the works were hurried on to completion, between June and October of 1730, 45,000 men worked on the building, and 1,286 oxen were bought to haul the heavy stones. The hospital built to accommodate the sick workmen cost 92,000,000 reis – about £20,000.

The palace is divided into two main parts : one to the east (560 by 350 feet), built round a large square court and devoted to the monks, containing the refectory, chapter-house, kitchen, a huge library, and cells for 280 monks. The other and more extensive part to the west comprises the King's apartments to the south, the Queen's to the north, and between them the church. The dimensions of the whole – 290,000 square feet – rival the

300,000 square feet of the Escurial. The refectory, 160 feet long, has hanging brass lamps, and, for tables, splendid slabs of Brazil wood. The library, 200 feet long, is one side secular and one side religious, with a separate space for the books of each different country. The inside of the church is of white marble, with pilasters of pink marble, and the altar paintings are by Trevisani. Finally, there are two towers 350 feet high, and a flat roof on which 10,000 soldiers could be reviewed. The clocks in the towers are set in motion by immense cylinders covered with spikes, there being upwards of 200 tons of metal in each tower. The works of the clocks, chimes, and bells were ordered in Holland, but the manufacturers refused to supply them, fearing that the kingdom of Portugal could not bear the charge. João V wrote back saying that he had made a mistake in the order and that he wished twice that amount to be incurred, and with his letter he prepaid all expenses.

That was Mafra ; and then, in an attempt to vie with his own records of extravagance, he went to the opposite extreme and spent as much money as possible on the smallest space practicable. This was a tiny chapel in the Church of São Roque at Lisbon. He had it designed and made in Rome, in 1742, by Vanvitelli (the architect of Caserta, near Naples). It has columns of lapis lazuli, alabaster pillars, balustrades of verde antique, mosaics made of agates ; and amethyst, ivory, and bronze are applied to the marbles. All the marbles and mosaics were prepared in Rome under Vanvitelli's supervision, while the best Italian silversmiths of the eighteenth century worked on the candelabra and the sacred vessels. The whole affair, when finished, was taken to pieces and brought to the coast at Ostia, where the Portuguese fleet met it and escorted it to Lisbon. On arrival, it was again put together and installed solemnly in place, the whole of this senseless extravagance being wasted on a space of some seventeen feet by twelve. The King's satisfaction from it was that he induced Benedict XIII to make the Cardinal of Lisbon into a Patriarch, and to allow him to officiate in vestments resembling those of the Pope, and his canons in imitation of those of the cardinals. Finally, in the last year of his reign, the title of " Fidelissimus," or " Most Faithful," was conferred upon him, to correspond with those of " Most Christian " and " Most Catholic," attributed respectively to the Kings of France and Spain.

Other, and dramatic, relics of this dead splendour are the Germain silver and the Royal coaches. The silver is now in the National Museum, but was formerly in the Necessidades Palace. There are more than a thousand pieces of it, in gold and silver plate and enamel ; breakfast services, dinner services, toilet-sets, centre-pieces for the table, and so forth. They are the work of the Germain family, and of other great French silversmiths, Cousinet and Godin. They give a fair idea of what must have been the fabulous luxury of this Court ; and the sight of the Royal coaches at Belem confirms these wildest hazards. The best of them are the Coronation coach of João V, which is decorated with tortoiseshell, and the coaches of the Marqués de Fontes, which were used in his embassy to Pope Clement XI in 1716. These have ivory fittings, curtains of gold brocade, and huge allegorical sculptures of Neptune and the sea-gods, in evocation of Portugal's past supremacy on the sea. Uniforms of indescribable magnificence were worn in these cavalcades, and as a public spectacle they must have been without parallel.

João V was also an admirer of music and the patron of

Caffarelli and Egizziello, the best castrati singers of the time. The palace choir was the finest body of singers in Europe. Operas were produced with great elaboration; for instance, in the best Portuguese native opera, the *Alessandro nell'Indie* of David Perez, which was dedicated to Caffarelli, a whole troop of horses appeared on the stage during the ballet and went through complicated manœuvres. The King's musical extravagance was on a par with his extravagance in building, or in negotiating with the Pope. An example of this was seen a few years ago, in London, by the writer of these pages. It was a magnificent red-lacquered harpsichord and its stool, which had been the gift of João V to a nun who was his mistress. It had only lately come out of the convent in Lisbon, where she lived, and its beauty illustrated that extraordinary and improbable period when the Bragança family, who should not have been any more important than, say, the King of Denmark, could dispose of all the gold and diamonds of Brazil.

Perhaps enough has been said about this improvident monarch, and, having given some outline of his achievement in spending so much money, it is time to turn from him to his people, and to the Church. There is a bewildering infinity of material, but practically no great names. In this fact, and in this fact only, is there any resemblance to Spain of the same date. There, also, the work was strictly local ; but, in Portugal, the conditions, and more especially the building material, were entirely different from anything to be met with in Spain. If the whole achievement, the King's buildings apart, could be summed up in a sentence, we should find these two things worthy of note ; the dark hard-stone churches and palaces of Oporto and its neighbourhood, and the use made by the Portuguese of azulejos. As this latter thing is universal to Portugal, it is best to consider it here before a detailed inventory is drawn up. The azulejos are found everywhere, Oporto and its district included, while this actual province, itself, can be discussed separately and in its place.

The Portuguese used coloured tiles to decorate the interiors of rooms and of churches, the walls of cloisters and staircases, the domes of churches ; even the exterior and the whole façade are treated in this way. The azulejo is the typical thing of Portuguese eighteenth-century architecture, and it is used on a scale that has no equal elsewhere, even in the mosques of Persia. The art was probably of Italian origin, and its earliest examples date from the beginning of the sixteenth century, but it became less and less Italian in style. It is usually blue and white, like Delft ware.

The amount of imagination put into this form of decoration is truly extraordinary. We find a church, at Oporto, with its whole façade one big composition of Carmelite nuns taking the veil ; there are open, monumental stairways lined with views of the town—this is at Braga ; cloisters with compositions running the whole way round, showing the life of an archbishop ; and, in other places, there are hunting and fishing scenes, the fables of La Fontaine, the four quarters of the world, battle scenes, naval battles, or bull-fights. In one or two places the azulejos are on a rose-coloured ground, and are of exceptional beauty. The whole of this form of expression is, as yet, unstudied and nearly unappreciated; but the effect of these azulejos is something so strange and fanciful that it hardly belongs to Europe.

The Portuguese seem always to have been haunted by
DA

their astounding maritime feats, which were the work, really, of one generation of men. They cannot get them out of their minds, and there is always an imaginary Orient at the back of their ideas. This is certainly the explanation of the Manoeline style, and the style of João V is not a bit less strange or remote from ordinary Western experience. In the Manoeline there are Moghul, Persian, Moroccan influences, and there is a digested memory of all this in the azulejos of this later date. Merely as a process it had, also, much to recommend it, being cheap in manufacture and always in the process of renewing its colours whenever there was rain. No one, who has not seen them, can imagine their delightful effect. The azulejos are a minor art used to enhance a minor architecture, but there are moments when an altogether exceptional poetry shines out of those china walls.

Some of the finest and earliest of the azulejos are to be seen at Bemfica, near Lisbon, in the villa of the Marqués de Fronteira. This is an Italian formal garden with statues and colonnades, and these latter are walled in superb manner with tiles that have a metallic lustre in them. There are two other places, near Lisbon, that are remarkable for their azulejo decoration. These are Oeiras, a little town on the sea, with a villa of the Pombal family that has a delightful formal garden and a fishing-pavilion with tiles of fishing-scenes, and the still more beautiful Cascata da Taveira, in which a waterfall is tamed and made to flow through the most enchanting china landscapes.

The other place is Queluz, and the palace there is an enchantment. It is one of the loveliest things of the entire eighteenth century, comparable to the Amalienburg and the finest triumphs of the Bavarian rococo style. It was built for Joseph I by native architects under the direction of a Frenchman, J. B. Robillon. The garden façade, and the side façades, with the staircases into the lower garden, are inimitable in their lightness and elegance. In the interior there is a room with tiles of a yellow ground and tropical trees bearing golden fruits. This is delightful; and so is another room papered with the Greek Wars of Independence, turbaned Turks, kilted Greeks, and Lord Byron, all in a landscape of Himalayan Mountains. The garden of the palace was, also, laid out by Robillon; it has beautiful fountains and statues and clipped hedges, and, as a climax, a river has been canalised into a tiled swimming-pool, and the bottom of this shows a huge blue fleet at full sail. This is a delicious feat of imagination; nothing cooler or more romantic could be thought of.

To return to Lisbon ; all there is left of our date can be put into a single paragraph. There is the Church of São Vicente de Fora, a good late sixteenth-century building by the Italian Filippo Terzi. The convent attached to this, which is the residence of the Patriarch of Lisbon, has very fine azulejos in its porch. They are battle-subjects, but all the passages, the staircases, and even the rooms, are decorated in this way. The cloisters show scenes from the fables of La Fontaine. None of the other churches are interesting ; and the palaces are too late in date, being built after the earthquake of 1755, to merit our attention. Typical of them is a palace by the architect Manuel da Costa Negreiros, near the above-mentioned church. This has a good interior staircase lined with tiles. But, in general, the domestic architecture in Lisbon is extremely disappointing. It is only the bright

colours of the coats of paint and the upward tilt of the
eaves, by which they are given a Chinese air, that make a
picturesque effect. Lisbon must be thought of, not as it
is now, but as it must have been before the earthquake.

The rest of Portugal is a different affair altogether,
as are, to this day, the country population compared with
the slum-dwellers of Lisbon. The country districts are
under-populated, and many small towns have enough
churches to accommodate three or four times their population. Traces of this feverish second period of building
are on every hand.

It has already been said that one centre of it is the
Algarve, and to this we may add the province of Alentejo,
so as to include all the country between Lisbon and the
Spanish frontier towards Seville. The whole of this is a
fascinating and unknown region ; and it has, outside our
subject, fine Roman remains, and glorious buildings of
the Gothic and Manoeline periods. In fact, it seems a
pity that our description of it must remain an appendix to
something that has not yet, itself, been properly described
as to its major and more important relics of a better period.
Our account must take the form of an itinerary. It is a
journey from Lisbon to the frontier, as if proceeding to
Huelvas, or Seville.

The first interesting town is Setubal, if we except the
Villa of the Dukes of Palmella passed on the way, at
Calhariz. Bacalhoa, built by the son of the great Albuquerque, we must reluctantly leave out of our narrative,
because it is removed by a century and a half from our
period. On the way to Setubal is the village of Vila
Fresca de Azeitão, of which the church has some of the
finest azulejos in Portugal. At Setubal there are some
fine things, but chiefly in the form of embellishments,

gold altar carvings, tile-panels, and so forth, to already existing churches. There is not much original work, so perhaps we can leave Setubal and make more directly for Evora, the metropolis of this whole region.

On the way there we pass Vendas Novas, another, and it will be the last, specimen of King João's handiwork. It is typical of him. A palace of fine stone was built there, with its complete equipment of furniture and comforts, to accommodate the Court for one night only on the occasion of the double marriage, in 1729, of his daughter, the Infanta Maria Josepha de Bragança, to Don Ferdinand, the eldest son of Philip V of Spain, while the Spanish Infanta, Marianna Vittoria de Borbon, was married to Dom José, the heir-apparent to Portugal. As there was no water near the palace, it was brought, at great expense, from a fountain made for the purpose at Pegões, where, also, the same king built another Quinta, or Royal villa. This palace, at Vendas Novas, still stands there, locked up and uninhabited, waiting for the Court to arrive again with its train of halberdiers and negro pages, with its fantastically garbed dwarves and its rhapsodists spouting impromptu verses as though in the worst throes of echolalia.

That romantic ruin is half way to Evora, and Evora is, perhaps, the most interesting town in the whole country. It is full of fine buildings of every date and period. The later houses have, in some cases, been decorated externally with graffitti drawings, and nearly all of them are tiled, or ornamented with mosaics of cut brick. The town is picturesque beyond imagination, with its Roman temple, its curious Moorish details, its local Gothic style, and its lack of any likeness to buildings seen before in any other country of Europe. Of our own period we must mention the choir of the cathedral and the capella-môr, which were entirely rebuilt by J. F. Ludwig, the architect of Mafra. Probably the most extraordinary collection of azulejos in Portugal are to be found in the buildings of the old University, a former Jesuit college. The entire structure is ornamented in this way, and in some of the halls the tile-compositions are the size of tapestries. There are more azulejos in the church of the Lóios monastery ; they portray the life of a bishop, with an abundance of characteristic detail. As to the palaces with graffitti decorations, the best of them are the ancient palace of the Inquisitors, now a hotel, and the palace of the Counts of Basto, where Catherine of Bragança lived as a widow.

Outside Evora, there are three interesting monasteries, that of d'Espinheiro, the Cartuxa, and São Bento de Castris. All these are of immense size, and have tiled cloisters, refectories, and chapels, and, after visiting them, it is not easy to distinguish them in the memory. However, it is a safe assertion that all three of them are a delight to the eye.

But it is certain that many charming things must be hidden in the district round Evora. Local guide-books at least mention the following : the Convent of São Paulo, near Redondo, in a forest on the slopes of a mountain, with fine azulejos ; the convent of Lóios, near the town of Arraiolos, which is famous for its eighteenth-century woollen-pile carpets (this again is a tiled church); and the village church of Brotas, near Mora, about forty miles from Evora, with its church completely panelled with azulejos. All of these must be delightful and charming.

If we go from Evora towards Badajoz, on the Spanish

frontier, the town of Estremoz gives us the Church of São Francisco, with its gilded woodwork and its double cloister, of which the staircase is finely ornamented with panels of tiles. There is also the Palacio Tocha, with azulejos depicting the Wars of Independence. Not far away is Borba, with glittering whitewashed houses, marble sills and lintels, and two convents, that of Servas and that of São Bartolomeu, both of them tiled, and the first of them having a fountain decorated with azulejos in the centre of its cloister.

Farther on is Vila Viçosa, the patrimony of the Bragança family, which has several churches notable for their tiles, notably the Esperança, the Conceição, and the Palace of the Bragança, which is a good, sturdy seventeenth-century building of three floors. There are, also, the convent of the Chagas, and that of the Augustinians, which contains the seventeenth-century pantheon of the ducal family.

Just on the frontier is the town of Elvas, from which the sugar-plums come. It is a prosperous snow-white town, with an extraordinary wealth of tiles. There is only space to mention the Church of Santa Clara, that of the Dominicans, the Jesuit college, the whole interior of the cathedral, more especially the sacristy, another Dominican church of octagonal plan with tiled cupola supported on painted and gilded columns, and the bishop's palace with its tiled staircases. The town of Elvas has an incredible profusion of picturesque detail, and it has fine wrought-iron balconies rather after the manner of those to be found in Syracuse and its region. Perhaps this mere catalogue of incident will show what there is to be seen there.

In the other direction from Evora, down towards the

Algarve, we pass Alvito, with a magnificent tiled church of 1647, and reach Beja. This has the convent of the Conceição, where the author of the famous *Portuguese Letters* was a nun. This has a cloister walled with green and white tiles with metallic lustre ; while the chapel of the hospital has tremendous Baroque gilding and wood-work in its interior. Far down to the south, near the Atlantic, is Loulé, a little town of absolutely blinding pallor from its whitewashed walls ; and, beyond this, Faro, with a good eighteenth-century cathedral, a bishop's palace with fine tiles, and the blue-and-white-tiled Church of São Francisco. Between Loulé and Faro is the village of Almancil, and this has a church completely covered, inside and out, with figured tiles.

This completes nearly all the objects of interest for our period in the Portuguese provinces south of Lisbon. Apart from Evora, it will be seen that the architecture is mostly a question of tile-work, but no one who has not seen them can realise the prodigal richness of their de-sign and their picturesque and transcendental effect. It puts them at a distance from anything else in Europe. This is, indeed, a neglected part of the world.

In Central Portugal there is Santarem. This has a Jesuit college with a tiled church, and the corridors of the monastery have magnificent azulejo compositions. Near Santarem is Almoster, with a tiled Bernardine monastery. Farther on is Tôrres Novas, with a tiled church, the Misericordia ; and the little town of Tancos, with two churches, the parish church and the Miseri-cordia. Both these are tiled. The town of Abrantes, interesting in other ways, has little or nothing of our period. Avis, the seat of the ancient military order, has the vast Baroque convent of the Benedictines, and another tiled parish church. Crato, still farther on, which was a priory of the Knights of Malta, has several fine houses of our date with coats of arms and wrought-iron balconies. So has another little place, Alter do Chão, and then we find ourselves at Elvas again, which has been already described. But there is another small district, just north of Elvas, which has plenty of material. There is Portalegre. This has the prodigious convent of the Conceição, with a fine façade, a court, a marble fountain, a tiled porch, and a tiled interior. There is, also, a Jesuit college with a dome of figured tiles, and the hospital of the Misericordia. The whole town is interesting. It is full of small palaces with blazoned fronts and projecting, pompous balconies. The cathedral is fine, too, more particularly its tiled sacristy with the inlaid vestment-presses. As for the little palaces, there are one or two streets nearly lined with them, but the best of them is the Palacio Amarelo, or Yellow Palace, with its splendid barred windows in the Spanish style and its marble staircase. The prefecture is fine, also ; it was formerly the palace of the d'Avilez. It has tiled staircases. There is, as well, the Liceu, formerly the Fonseca Acciaioli Palace, and its staircase has tiled panels of hunting-scenes.

This little part of Portugal is not yet finished. Near by is Castelo de Vide, another whitewashed town. This has more little palaces, and the Churches of Santa Maria, the Alegria, and São Tiago ; all have good tiles. The square of this town is entirely formed of eighteenth-century churches and palaces.

From this stage onwards we deal with Northern Portugal, though the character of the buildings is not yet that of the extreme north of the country, between Oporto and Vigo, where the best architecture of our date is to be found. At the same time, there is no longer the exuberance of the south. Two typical towns of this sort are Guarda and Viseu. These are, in other respects, about the most interesting little towns in the country – more especially Viseu, with its primitive pictures. They are high-lying towns, and a dark granitic stone is used side by side with the whitewashed walls of the south. This gives very picturesque contrasts. At Guarda there are several examples of small, town palaces with blazoned fronts and bold balconies. At Viseu the interest is more explicit in the Churches of the Carmo, São Bento, and São Miguel do Fetal, and in the palaces of the Rua Direita.

The centre of this whole region is Coimbra, but this town, which is almost a Toledo for its wealth of architecture, has only one first-rate achievement for us, and that is the library of the University. This compares with the Hofbibliothek of Vienna and the libraries of Melk and St. Florian, in the Danube Monasteries. It is a wonderful lacquered affair of green and gold, and red and gold. About fifteen miles from the town is the convent of Lorvão, which is a beautiful little thing with iron grilles, carved choir-stalls, and the silver tombs of two saints.

The most famous part of Portugal for architecture, which contains, in a small radius of miles, such amazing achievements as Batalha, Alcobaça, and Tomar, has nothing much to offer us. This is because of the indescribable splendour of what was already in existence in the days we are writing of ; but, if we go north towards Oporto, we find ourselves, at once, in another region full of the works we are searching for.

OPORTO : INTERIOR OF SANTA CLARA

OPORTO : INTERIOR OF SÃO FRANCISCO

There is, for instance, the convent of Lorical, not far from the seaport of Figueira da Foz. This was a nunnery of Poor Clares, built entirely in the eighteenth century. The church is completely lined with figured tiles, there are fine marble altars, and the capitals of the columns are of jasper. Perhaps the name of the architect, Manuel Pereira, is worth recording. Farther on, towards Oporto, is Aveiro. The convent of Jesus is the richest affair imaginable in the way of gilding, and it has fine tiles and a splendid wooden ceiling. There is, also, a good façade of granite to the Dominican church.

We are, now, so near to Oporto that it is better to proceed at once with our description of it. The town has one undoubted masterpiece – the circular Ionic cloister to the convent of Nossa Senhora da Serra do Pilar, which is on the promontory just across the Douro, opposite Oporto. The date of it is 1598, or 1600. It is a triumph over a very difficult problem, which is solved impeccably here, as it is nowhere else, except in Vignola's courtyard at Caprarola. In the town itself, the square of the Universidade has the two churches of the Carmo, one of which has an immense, external azulejo picture of Carmelite nuns taking the veil. This is one of the curiosities of the town. The interiors of the two churches are interesting, too, and the convent windows are remarkable. But the best thing in the town is São Francisco. The woodwork is curious beyond belief, with the vines trailing round the pillars, the ballet-figurants, and the elaborate altars like Bibbiena stage-scenes.

For the rest, an Italian architect, Nazzoni, worked at Oporto and helped to preserve that correct atmosphere which the wealth of the town was in danger of losing in such churches as that last described. He worked on the façade and the interior of the cathedral ; though, even here, the pagan spirit broke out and the cloister has tile-pictures of the Song of Songs and the Metamorphoses of Ovid. Nazzoni was also, perhaps, responsible for the façade of the Trinidade and for some of the private houses in Oporto. These are in restrained style, and often contain fine Chippendale furniture exchanged for port-wine with the English merchants of the place. It would seem to be almost certain that Nazzoni built the Palacio do Freixo, outside Oporto, a delightful and typical villa of the mid-eighteenth century, with terraces, statues, pavilions, and all the usual accompaniments of the kind.

But we can now leave Oporto for the northern province of Minho, which has many things to attract our notice, even at its first considerable town, Guimarães. Here there is the Church of São Francisco. There are the usual tiles, the usual gilded altars, and a fascinating sacristy full of mirrors, marble tables, and gilt furniture, with a fine ceiling. The town has several fine palaces, too, more especially the Vila Flor. Twenty miles away is the pilgrimage church of N.S. de Porto de Ave. It is an octagonal domed church, tiled inside, and with good fountains in its tree-shaded court. Even better than this is the Benedictine monastery of São Miguel de Refóios. It is near the town of Fafe. The monastery was entirely rebuilt two hundred years ago, and is in an extravagant rococo style, rather Bavarian in character, and certainly quite unlike the sober granitic buildings of the rest of the Minho province. The façade is fine, and flanked with two good towers.

On the direct line from Oporto to Braga the small town of Famalicão is passed. On a hill above it is the Church

Photo : Otto Schubert

BRAGA : PALACIO DEL MEJICANO

facing p. 61

of São Tiago de Antas, and this has a unique collection of
tiles on a rose background. They are in the choir of the
church, and there is nothing else like them in Portugal.
But Braga, only a dozen miles farther on, is one of the
great centres of Baroque art in Europe. The churches
and fountains are numberless ; it is very difficult to
compress all that must be said about Braga into a few
lines.
We will begin with the cathedral, just noting that it
has organ-cases and choir-stalls of our period in the coro
alto, and that two chapels contain remarkable azulejos
depicting an archbishop's life. The other churches are
entirely of our date. That of the Pópulo was built after
the plan of the Gesù in Rome, and given a new façade by
the architect Amarante, a century later. The azulejos in
the interior have as many characters as an American film.
Other churches are São Vitor, São Vicente, the Seminario
de Santo Antonio, and the Terceiros. The town hall has
a tiled staircase with views of the town, and all the above-
mentioned churches have azulejo compositions on an
unprecedented scale. The pictures are the size of
frescoes or tapestries. There are some fascinating small
palaces, the best being that called the Casa dos Biscainhos,
and the Palacio del Mejicano. This was built, presum-
ably, by a rich emigrant returned from Mexico. It is
perfectly proportioned and admirable in its dignity and
imagination, nicely bound-in, as it were, by the double
pilasters at each end of it, with elaborate windows, a
superb doorway, and balcony over it, and a balustraded
roof nicely broken with flaming urns. In fact, it would be
impossible to find a better small palace than this in any
town of Europe ; and there are several others, in Braga,
only just inferior to it.

Outside Braga there are several most interesting things. The pilgrimage church of Bom Jesus do Monte, which is the most famous of these, is hardly the most important. It is only the approach to it that captures the imagination, for this is up a Via Sacra of staircases and chapels leading to two immense staircases, profusely statued, and cooled with fountains. It makes a magnificent introduction to a disappointing church. The architect was Amarante. But, staircases and fountains apart, there are better things near Braga ; a few miles beyond this church there is a delicate and beautiful little rococo church of grey granite. It is the chapel of S.M. Madalena in the wild Serra da Falperra, and this is an extraordinary piece of elegance made out of the most intractable material. Then, just outside Braga, stands the old Romanesque abbey of São Frutuoso, which is but a small part of a Franciscan convent. The whole of the rest of the church is an especially fine example of Baroque planning. It has fine choir-stalls and organ-cases, and all about it is on a big and splendid scale. In another direction from Braga is the convent of the Tibães, which was the chief seat of the Benedictines in Portugal. There are four immense cloisters, one of them with the life of St. Benedict displayed in tiles all over its walls. The church is very fine rococo of an incredible delicacy. Last of all, about fifteen miles from Braga, is the Cistercian monastery of S.M. de Bouro. Its façade has life-size statues of the first Portuguese kings, done in a fascinating theatrical style similar to those in the Casa dos Reis at Alcobaça. They have periwigs, plumed hats, and scenic armour, and should be in a garden. Inside the church there are the usual huge azulejo compositions.

We will now deal with the outlying parts of the Minho

CAPELA DA FALPERRA (NEAR BRAGA)

province. Barcelos has two good things – its Benedictine church, finely tiled in the interior, and the octagonal domed church of the Senhor do Cruz. Outside the town is the Benedictine monastery of Vilar de Frades. This is a fine Baroque affair, and some of the chapels in the church have most curious azulejos of hunting-parties and bull-fights. Beyond Barcelos is Viana do Castelo, one of the most interesting towns in the country. This is crowded with fine things. There are the Church of São Domingo and that of the Misericordia, with azulejos by a famous craftsman, Policarpo d'Oliveira ; the huge Church of São Bento, with its choir-stalls and boiseries ; the Santuario de N.S. de Agonia of that Tuscan Baroque style that seems to be derived from Callot and from a study of bats ; and the Chapel dos Malheiros Reimões, which is attached to the fine palace of the same name. This is a little affair of the utmost grace and elegance. There are several good palaces, and at number 69 of the Largo de São Domingos a couple of rooms can be seen with the most enchanting tile-work depicting hunting and fishing scenes, the four quarters of the world, and receptions in aristocratic houses.

Between Viana do Castelo and the Spanish frontier towards Vigo there is little more ; but one other Portuguese province, that of Tras os Montes, remains to be described, and, on the way there from Oporto, the delightful small town of Penafiel is reached. This has two good churches, the Misericordia and the Ajuda, both of them with tiled towers. But it is in little palaces that Penafiel excels. The Rua Direita is one mass of them, and they present a most unlikely profusion of ideas for such a small, out-of-the-way place. The escutcheons are magnificent, and they give a really convincing idea of the owner's importance. There are good monastery churches near by, at Lousada and Travanca. The latter is a most ancient foundation in a beautiful wooded site. It has a fine cloister of the Tuscan order, and, in the sacristy, there are the most delightful vestment-presses, lacquered green and red, with chinoiserie figures.

Some twenty miles from Penafiel is the enchanting little town called Amarante. It is full of little houses of our period, all with balconies and coats of arms. As well as this, it has the Church of São Pedro, with a fine granite façade, tiled naves, and tiled sacristy, all of exceptional merit. But the pride of the town is the Church of São Gonçalo. An imposing granite façade, a dome tiled externally, resplendent woodwork and choir-stalls, a cloister of Ionic pilasters and columns carrying vases, and with a Persian-looking decoration of blue tiles on its walls ; last, because it is best of all, a most splendid organ-case upheld by carved tritons – these few things must serve to give some idea of Amarante, for there is no space for more.

Farther on, and a few miles from the railway, is Lamego. Here we find work by the Italian Nazzoni, from Oporto. He remodelled the cathedral. There are also in this town, the bishop's palace, that of the Peixotos Padilhas, and the pilgrimage church of N.S. dos Remedios, an affair rather after the manner of Bom Jesus do Monte. Right at the end of this railway line, and only a mile or two from the Spanish frontier, there stands the old Bernardine abbey of Santa Maria d'Aguiar, which is said to contain, in addition to its earlier work, some good azulejos, a cloister of the Tuscan order, and fine choir-stalls.

In another direction, going north from Lamego

LAMEGO : SANTUARIO DOS REMEDIOS (EXTERIOR STAIRWAY)

towards Galicia, the first town is Vila Real, another of the
intensely picturesque small Portuguese cities. Nearly
every house is old, and a great many of them date from
our period. The outstanding things in it are the Church
of the Clerigos, with azulejo panels ; the cathedral, which
has some late details; the Convent of Santa Clara, covered
all over with azulejos; the Church of São Pedro, also
with azulejos ; and, finally, the Church of São Paulo,
which has two great Trajanic columns outside it after the
style of the Karlskirche in Vienna. A mile or two from
the town, at Mateus, is the villa of the local nobleman, the
Conte de Vila Real, and this is the finest country-house
and garden in Portugal. The villa, itself, has an excellent
façade, with two projecting wings, and a balustraded,
pinnacled, and statued roof.

The terminus of this particular line is Chaves ; and
this contains the parish church, which has fine choir-
stalls and organ-cases, and the Church of the Misericordia,
with its striking façade of granite, composed of three
balconies and of twisted Salomonic pillars. The whole
interior is treated with figured azulejos. There is, also, a
most curious building, the octagonal Church of São João
de Jesus. It is domed, and has a granite façade taken up,
mostly, by two angels swinging a censer.

Only one more town need be described – Bragança,
which was the ancient fief of the family of that name.
Here, there are the churches of São Vicente and the
Convent of the Clares. Azulejos adorn both these
churches, but the town, in spite of its having a famous
name, is not to be compared with Lamego, with Vila Real, or
with Penafiel, or Amarante. All four of those are an enchantment, and, indeed, after the great revelation of Tomar
and of Batalha, these small towns, with never a population

EA

of more than seven or eight thousand, are the most beautiful things in the country. They compare very favourably with anything of the kind in Spain or Italy, while they are nearly as unknown to present-day travellers as the towns in Arabia or Abyssinia.

LAMEGO : SANTUARIO DOS REMEDIOS (COURT OF THE KINGS)

III

MEXICO

THIS is such an immense subject that anything approaching a complete inventory of its effects is quite impossible. There is hardly a country, anywhere in the world, so full of churches and monasteries. The first buildings were the work of Franciscan friars. They were semi-fortified, for Mexico was hardly safe yet. They were solid, sober, dogmatic ; and it was only in the next century, when the other religious orders arrived, that a national character began to form itself and to find its expression in architecture. New Spain was now a hundred years old. It had begun to be a country.

Before this, the Spanish buildings in the New World had followed traditional lines. The Church of San Francisco at Cholula was of definitely Gothic type, while the Capilla Real, in the same town, with its sixty-four columns and forty-nine domes, was modelled, beyond doubt, upon the mosque at Cordoba. On the other hand, the hurriedly converted Aztecs showed their race plainly enough in the carvings and decorative detail.

The end of the sixteenth and beginning of the seventeenth centuries were a time of great activity, and the contemporary Spanish Plateresque style appears in many Mexican examples, more especially at San Agustin Acolman, near Texcoco. This is as fine as the Hospital of Santa Cruz at Toledo, or as any of the Plateresque buildings in Spain. It might well be the work of Berreguete, or Enrique de Egas. The country got more and more rich with the discovery of new gold and silver mines. With the coming of the late Baroque and the Churriguerresque styles the Mexicans had money enough to attempt anything, and this strange mood of architecture is on the threshold of the most extraordinary developments it ever underwent. There was prodigious energy. For this newly discovered form ran into so many new directions that all its best examples may be said to be a style in themselves that defies classification and demands treatment as a separate manifestation. The small examples of it are as interesting as the big ones. Nearly every Indian village in Central Mexico has a domed church, and there are many little towns, so small that they have no place on the map, which are to be seen at the foot of a cluster of domes that would be the pride of any city in Spain or Italy.

The subject is too enormous and copious for any detailed treatment, and the only solution is to describe some selected examples. The cathedral in Mexico City is not included in these, partly because it is of earlier date, and partly because it is the one building which is sure to be seen by anyone who visits the country. Information about it would be superfluous, and it is more important to add to what is unknown and to indicate some few of the buildings in other towns.

The particular character of the places to be described rests upon features which can be found nowhere else. The brilliantly tiled domes, the varying colours of the external walls, the polychrome interior decorations — these are things that do not occur in any other architecture of the Baroque period. But they have so marked an individuality, and are so completely different each from the other, that it would be useless to generalise about

MEXICO CITY : CATHEDRAL AND SAGRARIO METROPOLITANO

facing p. 68

them, and the only course is to discuss each separate example as it arises.

We will begin with one or two examples, other than the cathedral, in Mexico itself, and the first of them shall be the Sagrario Metropolitano, which is a separate parish church, though joined on to the cathedral. This is one of the best Churriguerresque buildings in all Mexico. It dates from 1749. The most remarkable things about it are the two façades. It is built after the plan of a Greek cross. The centre above this is domed, and the two façades decorate the nave and transept. They are of the richest possible carving ; statues stand upon the most elaborate brackets, and are, themselves, sheltered in ornate niches. The corner between the two façades has an elaborate stone door, and then walls of a wonderful red tezontle, the favourite building material of Mexico, rise up in a flight of bold and increasing curves, that are edged with a trimming of white stone, until they join on with the façades at either hand. The red tezontle walls are further ornamented with the most beautiful windows in the same white stone, and these are in Sicilian, or Leccese, style. The architect of this extremely successful, skilful, and picturesque building was Lorenzo Rodriguez. His two façades are masterpieces in their way ; their balance, although they are different in detail, is perfect. Indeed, the sight of these two façades and their red tezontle connecting wall, with the elaborate door at the angle and the façades declining away on either side, is the finest thing in the town. Unfortunately, the interior of the church was completely ruined early in the present century, and its immense Churriguerresque altars and reredoses have practically disappeared, having been melted down, as likely as not, for the gold they contained.

There is another church by the same architect, Lorenzo Rodriguez, in Mexico City. It is that of La Santisima. This is later in date, being completed in 1783, and has another characteristic façade, of three stories, framed by an infinity of pilasters and inverted pyramids. A huge relief of the Holy Trinity takes up the centre of the middle story, and all the details are formed from the Papal insignia. The summit of the tower is made out of the triple crown of the Papacy. The side-walls, again, are built of red tezontle, and the dome is of glazed tiles set in a reddish surface. There is an exquisite side-door. The interior in this church, also, has been completely gutted.

The third church in Mexico City that it is necessary to consider is that of Santo Domingo. This was finished a little earlier, in 1733. It is made of a porous stone which is a light wine-red in colour. In this instance, it is the interior that is interesting, for it has retained most of its Churriguerresque altars. But this church, also, is the mere wreck of its former self. Nearly the whole of its convent has been demolished ; the cloisters have gone, the gardens have been destroyed, and so has a chapel by Lorenzo Rodriguez that once stood in the grounds.

The only other building we need notice in the city is the Casa de los Mascarones. Immense sums were lavished on this by its owner, Don José de Mendoza, Conde del Valle de Orizaba. At his death, in 1771, it was still unfinished ; and it is an interesting link in architectural history, for this strange palace is absolutely similar in style to the Seminario and the Prefettura of Lecce. No eyes that have seen the one could fail to think of the other. It is a one-storied building, of some eight windows, broken by elaborate masked pilasters.

MEXICO CITY : ONE OF THE TWO FAÇADES OF THE
SAGRARIO METROPOLITANO

The central doorway is a fine composition, too, and it is much to be regretted that the rich nobleman who built it should have never lived to complete the whole palace.

Before we finish with Mexico City, mention must be made of the Capilla del Pocito, the " Chapel of the Holy Well," some three miles outside the town. It is one of the most famous pilgrimage centres in the world, and the chapel built above this well is among the finest architectural designs in the country. The architect was Don Francisco Guerrero Torres, and the date of it is 1777–1791. The plan is formed by the principal chapel, which is elliptical, and by a small circular chapel annexed to it, which actually covers the holy well. There is a small sacristy at the back, in addition. Both the big and the little chapels are domed, and they are tiled in a chevron pattern of blue and white, with the ribs of the domes in chrome yellow. Above the domes are lanterns, alike in shape, and also tiled with the same colour-scheme.

The principal doorway is curved in plan, following the ellipse of the building. It is in two stories, with Corinthian columns. The side-doors are, also, curved, but with strange, flat Salomonic pillars, of a bastard Doric order. The windows, above, and all the side-windows in the lower parts of the chapel, are given the symbolical shape of a star.

The great point of this building is in the contrast of its lower part, built of red tezontle with its star-shaped windows of white stone, against the two domes of blue and white tiles. The tezontle walls are, indeed, almost maroon in colour. The whole thing is a most daring and successful exploitation of new colour-schemes. More than this, it is one of the outstanding creations of late Renaissance architecture, and when its date is considered it becomes the more remarkable.

We will now move away from the capital to the city of Puebla, a journey of one hundred and thirty miles. This is the centre of an extremely individual style of building, and it is one of the most picturesque towns in the world. Three snow-crowned volcanoes, Popocatapetl, Iztaccihuatl, and Malinche, look down upon it.

The cathedral is, perhaps, an even finer building than that at Mexico City, but it belongs to the early seventeenth century, and is not in our province for that reason. But its other churches—and there are many of them—are experiments in a style that is to be met with nowhere else.

The unique feature in it is the use made of coloured tiles. These were a speciality of Puebla from an early date, for it is believed that potters from Talavera, in Spain, settled here soon after the Conquest. By the middle of the eighteenth century it is said that there were no less than thirty of these tile-factories established in the city. It has even been stated that Chinese workmen were imported, but this is evidently untrue, and the originality of the designs is simply due to local, and native, inspiration. What can only be described as a china architecture was invented, and it excels over the uses made by the Portuguese of azulejos in the fact that it was no mere figured decoration of blank, level spaces but a definite part of an architectural plan.

Every detail in this town is of utmost beauty, and as though displayed by the cleverest scenic painter of whom the imagination can conceive. Even the plain whitewashed walls are miraculous in their colour-shading, though this is the sun and the climate and not the direct work of human hands. Every opportunity, though, is put

GUADALUPE: CAPILLA DEL POCITO

GUADALUPE : CAPILLA DEL POCITO (DETAIL)

to unrivalled use, and the builders of common houses were, so to speak, masters in daylighting. The shops where pulque is sold are decorated, even in modern times, with the most excellent wall-paintings, more especially of bull-fights, which, alone, are worth collecting in a book. All in all, it is difficult to think of a more congenial city than Puebla, for every step taken in it is a fresh delight to the eyes.

The Church of Guadelupe is an excellent example of the Pueblan style. Its colour-scheme is of great elaboration. In the façade, on either side of the main doorway, it has zigzag bands of tiles in orange, blue, and green alternating with white. The arched frontispiece is of blue and white. The figures of angels in the spandrels have yellow dresses and orange wings. The two towers are of red and green tiles, and the four tiled pictures with polychrome figures have blue and white borders. Above these are the sun and moon, in tiles, with orange bodies and yellow rays upon a blue ground. The interior of the church has been miserably gutted of all its former display ; but perhaps these details of the façade may give some idea of its brilliant, reverberating effect.

Another church, the Templo de San Francisco, has a façade of extreme originality. The glazed tiles are set in red brick ; and at places there are flower-pictures in blue and yellow lustre on a white ground. In the middle, there is an elaborate entrance rising up in four stages past this glitter of colour. It is a magnificent and wonderful conception, and the façade bends forward and advances at each side, carrying a repeat of these tile patterns.

All of these churches are different from each other. There is no monotony among them. That of San José has a treatment of blue and yellow ; its dome is yellow, blue, and orange. The house where the parish priest lives has a dome of white tiles with blue designs upon them ; bands of yellow tiles as ribbing to the dome ; and a lantern of white and light blue alternating with yellow and dark blue.

These are the churches with the best exteriors, but some of those in the town are of equal importance for their internal decoration. That of San Christobal has wonderful stucco work ; the Soledad has two enormous Churriguerresque gilded altars ; Santa Catarina has no less than eight of these, and they tower up, with all their figurants, as in a theatrical finale, to the roof of the church. Still more churches – the Templo de la Compania, San Marcos, La Santisima – are all interesting, and nearly all of them have the typical Pueblan marquetry work, in the way of confessionals, pulpits, or choir-stalls.

This evocation of so much brilliance and colour leaves it to be understood that the villages and small towns in the neighbourhood have their full share of interest. It is, indeed, probably the most interesting part of Mexico. Its absolute differentiation from the type of building common in the Valley of Mexico shows the extreme adaptability and variety of style that could be evolved from this supposedly decadent architectural form. Actually, there can seldom have been so much vitality expressed in brick and stone. The beauty of the natural setting, of course, enhances its effects, but for carefully planned gaiety and exuberance Puebla is a town that has no parallel.

We will now examine a third, and entirely different, manifestation which is peculiar in two things – that it is all the work of one man, and that this architect lived till 1833, when architecture had been dead, in Europe, for

PUEBLA : SAN FRANCISCO ACATEPEC

PUEBLA : SAN FRANCISCO

at least sixty years. His name was Francisco Eduardo Tresguerras, and he was born at Celaya in 1745. He was a Creole, or native-born Mexican of Spanish blood. As well as architect he was sculptor and painter ; he was even musician and poet as well. Nearly all his architectural work is to be found in the two towns of Queretaro and Celaya. Queretaro is another town of this exuberant Southern character, which is only marred by the fact that the execution of the Emperor Maximilian took place in it. In the time of Tresguerras it had already one fine church – that of San Agustin, built by the two Augustinian monks Luis Martinez Lucio and Carlos Benito de Butron Moxica. It stands on a platform reached by seven steps, and perhaps the most curious thing about it is the unfinished tower. This is carved elaborately in a kind of flat bas-relief, and it comes to a sudden end just above the knees of the huge statues at each corner of it. They look like the legs of dancers, and at the side of the dome, which is glazed with blue and white tiles, there are seated figures, archangels in heroic costume, in breastplates and profusely feathered hats ; while, at each corner of the dome, there are the more than life-size figures of angels, who wear enormous plumes on their heads and are like Indian caciques executing a pagan dance.

The cloister is more curious still. Between each pair of arches the pillar that acts as the separating bar between them has been made into a caryatid. The cloister has two stories, and, in consequence, two tiers of caryatids. They are all different ; some are bearded patriarchs, others are aquiline Indians or laughing fauns. In the upper story they are holding their giant hands with the fingers outstretched to full height above their heads, in order to support the arch for which each hand is responsible. All this time they are making signs to each other. They are talking in the deaf and dumb language. If Queretaro had already a church as queer as this, it made a good soil for an imaginative genius of the scale of Tresguerras. He took full advantage of it, and in the two convents of Santa Rosa di Viterbo and Santa Clara he produced the most perfect and complete examples of the Churriguerresque style to be found anywhere in the world. An enormous sum of money, realised out of the merchandise seized from *contrabandistas*, had been placed at the disposal of the Convent of S. Rosa di Viterbo. In both these churches the choir-screens and the screened balconies for the Mother Superior have assumed an extraordinary importance as decoration. In that of S. Rosa the balcony for the Mother Superior has its elaborate golden base supported by the carved retablo of an altar. The confessionals are designed in keeping with the rest of the colour-scheme, so that their gilding is sharpened with shrill touches of metallic lustre, an effect which is obtained in the mediæval fashion, by mixing the colours with a transparent varnish medium applied over a ground of gold-leaf. In this way, ruby and emerald green effects of great violence and beauty are obtained. His use of colour is seen all over the building. The reredos of the altar of S. José has its picture by Miguel Cabrera (the Zapotec Indian, the greatest Mexican painter, and the master of Tresguerras) framed with garlanded lines that are treated in emerald, making a beautiful contrast with the rich gold masses about them. The pulpit is a superb piece of inlay in ivory, tortoiseshell, and mother-of-pearl, the tortoiseshell being underlaid with thick gold leaf.

The sacristia has the best painting by Tresguerras. It

is the Hortus Conclusus, a symbolisation of Santa Rosa, in which lambs are given white roses by the Virgin and bear them to the feet of the Cross, to be turned red by the blood from Christ's wounds. An angel with a vase of roses and lilies holds it to the Saviour's side, so that the water falls upon the white lilies and the blood upon the red roses. At the same time, it shows the nuns and their pupils at work in the garden of the convent.

The convent church of Santa Clara, compared with this, is a little more rococo, a little more in ordinary experience. Only the church now remains. The convent used to cover several acres of ground, and was the home of as many as eight thousand nuns. The church has a splendid tiled dome. It is blue on a yellow ground, like the smaller dome of the lantern ; the base is of white and blue. The lowest belt of the tower has a pattern of blue and white on yellow and light green ; the two middle belts are blue, yellow, and white below, and blue and white above ; the dome of the tower being blue and white over a belt of yellow and white.

The interior is smaller than that of S. Rosa, but is even richer in decoration. The balcony of the Mother Superior stands like a bridge over a richly carved doorway below, and a splendid reredos, on the opposite wall, is designed as a pendant to it. The whole of this huge building was designed by Tresguerras, who was responsible for all the details, and supplied rough sketches, even, from which the best of his band of sculptors, Mariano Arce and Mariano Perusquia, carved their figures. There are six immense Churriguerresque altars, among the finest of their kind in Mexico. This peculiarly Spanish invention is here carried to unparalleled lengths, and their effect is the most magnificent thing that can be imagined. It is difficult to believe they are eighteenth-century work ; they seem to belong to the century of Gil de Siloe and the retablos of Burgos Cathedral and the Cartuja de Miraflores.

These two churches, taken together, must represent almost the richest phase of decoration that has ever occurred, and Tresguerras, having completed them, turned in another direction and built the Church of El Carmen, at Celaya. This was begun as late as 1803, and is a masterpiece of pure late classical design, almost incredible as having come from the same hand that designed these two convents. Instead of pseudo-Greek, he adopted a classical Renaissance manner. It has a beautiful dome, elliptical in plan, with eight windows in the drum, separated by Corinthian columns in pairs. It is tiled in alternating yellow and green. The tower is a tremendous classical invention. The interior contains statues, paintings, and three large frescoes by this extraordinary man. There can be little doubt that this Church of El Carmen is not only the best church of the nineteenth century, but, also, the last good church ever built.

Tresguerras is buried, near by, in the Church of San Francisco, where he designed his own mortuary chapel. It has a frieze of the Twelve Apostles by him, a crucifix from his hand, and signed manuscript poems by him hang upon the walls. During his lifetime he had been Sindico, Regidor, and Alcalde of his native city.

Other buildings by Tresguerras are two palaces and the formal garden of the main plaza in Celaya, the tower and church of S. Agustin, and the huge, five-spanned bridge leading to Celaya over the river Laja. This has four great stone finials at each end, on either baluster, and the bridge was specially planned so that from its centre there was a view of his dome to the Church of El Carmen. It is said, also, that he designed the great Teatro Alarcon in the mining-town of San Luis Potosi, and painted the scenery for it.

Another most typical Mexican town is Oaxaca, and before we come to the last three or four supreme examples, which must be considered at greater length, it would be convenient to group Oaxaca with another town of the same type. In Oaxaca, the best thing is the monastery of Santo Domingo, and its culmination in the domed vaulting of the organ-loft, which is an enormous tree extending its branches and leaves of gold in every direction, between which there are the busts of saints, diminishing in size as the height increases, until, at the apex, only the faces are shown. Other churches in Oaxaca are La Soledad, with a façade of brown stone, and the Church of San Felipe, in green stone, with some tremendous Churriguerresque altars. This is the most southerly town of any interest in Mexico. San Luis Potosi is in the other direction, in the north of the country. This has the Church of El Carmen, with domes tiled in blue, green, yellow, and white, and a huge poly-chrome reredos designed by Tresguerras. Guadalajara, Morelia, Cuernavaca, all have interesting things of our date. Zacatecas has its Jesuit Church of Santo Domingo, with Churriguerresque altars and an octagonal sacristy, but there is no space to delay over these, and we must get to our four or five culminating examples.

They are the finest things in the country, and, although their date is in each instance approximately the same, they present the utmost difference of treatment. Their rich-ness is beyond parallel ; but so much ornament is always balanced by quiet, blank spaces of wall. An untrained observer would without hesitation ascribe them to a date two centuries earlier than their reality, for they are, in a sense, neo-Plateresque in treatment.

We will begin with the Church of San Cayetano, two miles outside Guanajuato. This is a town that attained great importance and wealth in the eighteenth century with the discovery of a huge vein of silver running under the city. The church stands on a hill above the town, and all the hillsides about it are pitted with mine-shafts and ore-heaps. Guanajuato, itself, has at least two fine churches, the Jesuit Church, La Compañia, and the smaller church of San Diego that has a really magnificent Churriguerresque façade.

But it is San Cayetano, outside the town, that is the important thing. This was built for the great Valenciana silver-mine by its proprietor, the Conde de Rul. It was completed as late as 1788. During the years of its productivity, the output of this mine was eight hundred million dollars ; now it is worked out, the village has shrunk back into a miserable hamlet, and the church is in the charge of one lonely priest. In the days of its plenty, the scale of extravagance on which it was built can be indicated by the temporary ornament that was provided for the ceremony of dedication, for the tissue that entered into its composition cost three hundred Mexican dollars a yard.

A service of fabulous magnificence used to be supported there by the contribution of all the thousands of miners employed in the Valenciana mine. Each one of them gave, every week, the value of a piece of ore called *piedra de mano* – a stone the size of the hand. This produced fifty thousand dollars a year. The

TEPOZOTLAN : SEMINARIO DE SAN MARTIN I

facing p. 81

TEPOZOTLAN : SEMINARIO DE SAN MARTIN II

TEPOZOTLAN : SEMINARIO DE SAN MARTIN III

facing p. 81

splendour of the vestments and the sacred vessels may be imagined.

The façade is of a beautiful golden stone. The chief doorway and the side-doors are wonderful designs ; indeed, no mason of our times could be found who would embark upon their translation into stone. The interior is white, or white on a straw-coloured ground, and there is a splendidly inlaid pulpit of Queretaro work. But the unique possessions of the church are its three Churriguerresque altars, great golden towers in height. Their intricacy is quite extraordinary. There are as many figures standing on pilasters and niches as there are sailors when the yards are manned on a warship.

The next church to be described – that of Tepozotlan – is more interesting still. Its correct name is the Seminario de San Martin, and it was built as a country retreat for the Jesuits. Though deep in the country, the place is easy enough of access, being just on the edge of the Valley of Mexico, near Teoloyucan, and only some thirty-five miles from Mexico City.

The church was built as early as 1504, but, nearly two hundred years later, the new façade was added and the interior was redecorated. The convent was, naturally, dissolved eighty years ago, at the time of the confiscation of all the monasteries ; but, being Jesuit, and not strictly monastic, it was still, until at any rate a couple of years ago, in the hands of that order. In consequence, the church is splendidly kept up, unlike nearly every other institution in the country.

The façade and the tower have been arranged with a consummate scenic sense, for the great central doorway has plain surfaces on either side of it, and these set off the decoration in splendid fashion. The façade is in three

FA

stories. The first cornice has a level flat line, like a breathing-space, and above it the second story begins, and ends in slightly more broken lines at its cornice. Above that, the third story climbs up in successive spurts, like the jets of a fountain. All of this can be seen to greatest advantage through the wall that surrounds the monastic estate, for this has inverted circular capping – reversed arches, that is to say. These are the symbols of ecclesiastical authority, and, at the same time, they provide the loop-holes through which the façade can best be seen.

The tower, also, is a fantastic success. It is in two great stories with a domed lantern. Each face of the tower has corner pilasters, so that there are always two pilasters seen at every angle.

Inside the church, there is equal magnificence. The floors of all the chapels are in glazed tiles of yellow, blue, and white, and above this chequered field rise the huge carved altars, like knights and castles ready to move. The camarin is the most splendid example of its class in Mexico, but, first of all, the purpose of a camarin must be explained, as they are to be found nowhere else. They are a kind of boudoir in which the vestments for the image of the Virgin are kept, and where the image is dressed with an elaborate ceremony. The camarin at Tepoztlan has, to begin with, a domed ceiling lighted by a triple lantern. These following colours flash out, one after another, gold, scarlet, blue, light and dark green, and silver, all of them obtained out of the metallic lustre. For the rest, the camarin has the usual inlay on doors and presses ; there are huge panels of wood-carving, big groups of polychrome sculpture, and great oil-paintings framed in panels. It has, also, the most graceful stone

TLAXCALA : SANTUARIO DE OCOTLAN

facing p. 83

stoups for the holy water, beautiful compositions in almost a Renaissance manner.

The actual lantern to the dome of this camarin is in three stories. From each of the two lower stories, heads of cherubs, angels, and saints lean out, sculptured in relief. The light from the windows in these two stories is modified by screens, but from the third and highest floor the full illumination is admitted, so that the emblem of the Espiritu Santo, the white dove upon a ground of azure, seems to be floating upon a veritable sea of light.

We have now arrived at our penultimate specimen, the Santuario de Ocotlan, a mile outside the town of Tlaxcala, which place is some eighty-five miles from Mexico City. It is, in many respects, the most extraordinary of the whole series, being absolutely unique and unlike anything else, though it may be worth noting that the delightful parish church of Tlaxcala is, almost certainly, by the same hand. The dimensions of the church are very small. It is no more than a small nave, and on three of its sides it is attached to other buildings in such a manner that it has only got the one façade where the doorway is. But there are two towers flanking this.

The façade and the tops of the towers are of a dazzling white. The base of the towers, from the top of the façade downwards, so that they frame it in, are of scarlet glazed bricks set in brilliant white mortar, and shaped like the meshes of a net. The effect is of scarlet shagreen.

The doorway is two stories high. The first story is formed by the door and by two pilasters on each side, with, between each pair, a pedestal carrying the figure of a winged archangel. Above these are busts of the Fathers of the Church. The cornice is like the finest Renaissance work ; and these pillars supporting it are altogether detached from the wall. The second story is formed by a window shaped like a double star, with, in front of its light, a statue of St. Francis holding three globes that support a statue of the Virgin. On either side are pillars, similar to those below, with more winged archangels. Above the window, the cornice meets again and supports yet another trio of archangels. Behind all this, there is an immense recessed shell, springing right out to roof the figures below.

The towers are in two stories, also. They consist of Salomonic pillars, and the second story is still further strengthened by the addition of obelisks. This gives a slight effect of heaviness and overhang to the towers, but it was done on purpose, so as to accentuate their height when seen immediately from below, out of the shadow thrown by the giant shell.

In effect, this façade and its towers are indescribable. Their appearance against the glittering blue of the Mexican sky must be left to the imagination. It is snowy white and scarlet shagreen against the intense blue of space.

Luckily, the interior of this church is no detraction from the splendid impression left by its façade. Nothing whatever has been destroyed. The great feature of it is the treatment of the transept and chancel as a single unit, separated from the body of the church by a construction that resembles a theatre proscenium. The whole space between the end of the aisles and the altar is given this theatrical flavour. There are huge gilded retablos reaching right up to the ceiling, and the golden glitter and droop of their ornament make this open space like a grotto, at the back of which, through the huge open proscenium, the high altar appears like the stage.

The whole of this grotto, with its carved walls, the

drooping stalactites among the figures of saints, and the roof inlaid with precious woods, was the work of a pure-blooded Indian, Francisco Miguel, who spent twenty-five years of his life on the work. Leading out of this part of the church is the camarin, upon which Francisco Miguel spent the remainder of his years, and, to judge from the amount of work it contains, his life must have been healthy and protracted. The decoration is gold and green on white, with other brilliant colours used as accent. The dome has a blue ground, with a circle of gold on scarlet. A circle of polychrome Apostles stands round a blue ground, in the act of receiving tongues of flame from the Holy Spirit, symbolised by a white dove in the centre. The feet of the Apostles stand on a white and gold cloud. The altar beneath the dome is of silver, and the figure of the Virgin is of pure gold, while all the walls, doors, cupboards and presses are carved and in-laid by this pure-blooded Indian. The floor, of inlaid marbles, is covered with a piece of ancient Mexican figured tapestry.

The church which we have reserved till last, and will now describe, is the finest and culminating work of Baroque art in the New World. It is the Church of San Sebastian y Santa Prisca, in the little town of Taxco, a most inaccessible place, being five hours' ride on horse- or mule-back over the mountains from Iguala, which town is some hundred and forty-five miles from Mexico City. From Iguala to Taxco is a dangerous and pre-cipitous journey. It is a tumbling, hilly country of red stone, rich in minerals, for the first silver sent from New Spain to Europe was mined here in 1522 ; and the only historical fact connected with Taxco is that it was the birthplace of the Spanish poet and dramatist, Alarcon.

The church was built by the mine-owner, José de la Borda, about 1757, in gratitude for the success of his mining ventures. He had come as a young boy, penniless, from Bordeaux, and made a colossal fortune from the silver-mines of Taxco. His intention was to repay this by the erection of the most splendid church in the Western world.

It stands in a plaza that is almost the only level ground for a huge distance round. The little town, itself, has great character, and is so full of old houses that the whole place has been recently declared a national monument. No wheeled traffic can pass through the steep streets, owing to their narrowness, and they are paved with pebbles laid level from house and house and ornamented in mosaic patterns. The church lies at the top of the town.

It has two towers and a dome of blue, orange, green, and white tiles. The material of the church is a hard and fine-grained brown stone. There is a most fantastic façade of two stories, with pairs of Salomonic pillars in the second of them. The window usually placed in that position is here occupied by a great bas-relief, and the window is placed above it. The towers, on either side, are given a plain treatment as far as the top of the façade. Their only ornament is four windows in each, one above another, of a fine and capricious rosette design. Above this, the towers break into great elaboration, and are in two stories. All four faces of each two floors are decorated with balconies that are supported by leering, sardonic masks.

Inside the church there are no less than twelve gilded Churriguerresque altars. Such an array of them exists nowhere else in the world. They are gold in background,

TAXCO : SAN SEBASTIAN Y SANTA PRISCA   I

facing p. 86

TAXCO : SAN SEBASTIAN Y SANTA PRISCA II

but with polychrome sculptures and polychrome accents.
All the mural decoration of the church was the work of
one painter, a pure-blooded Zapotec Indian, and the best
painter of the Mexican school, Miguel Cabrera (1695–
1768). All the altar paintings are by him, as well. The
sacristy, which is a magnificent room, has eight huge
panels by his hand. It is filled with the most elaborate
and fanciful chairs and tables that can be imagined. Next
to this is the sala capitular, in which there are portraits
of de la Borda and other great dignitaries, also by Cabrera.
All the appurtenances of the church were of the most
splendid quality. The custodia given by de la Borda, and
made of gold and jewels, is easy enough of access, since
it is now in the treasury of Notre-Dame, at Paris.

The blaze and glitter of the twelve great altars is
beyond description. Great reliefs in gold fill the pen-
dentives of the interior of the dome. There are a pulpit
and two confessionals carved in a dark wood, and the
floor of the church used to be entirely covered with a
superb great India carpet imported to Taxco by way of
Manila and Acapulco. A fragment of this is still in use,
as a rug, in the sacristy.

Such is this church, described in the baldest and most
uncompromising reality, but it would be impossible to do
justice, in words, to the majesty and fantasy of its appearance. Not only is it the finest thing in Mexico, but
it ranks with the greatest achievements of Baroque art in
Europe. It is better than anything in Spain, with the
exception of the cathedral at Santiago da Compostella,
and it would be hard to find anything in Italy that is better
than this church at Taxco. This applies, also, to all
three of the churches described just before it. La
Valenciana, Tepozotlan, Ocotlan, Taxco – these are four

churches with the omission of which no history of architecture is complete. They are delightful things, not to be solemnly appreciated, but to be liked for the confidence and exuberance that inspired them. If this is allowed them, they have a supremacy that no other buildings can challenge. When we add to them the pair of convents at Queretaro and the churches of Puebla, there seems to be an authentic reason for Mexico being called the New Spain.

IV

SOUTH AMERICA

THIS has proved to be a most disappointing field of enquiry, because the monuments are there but it is the information about them that is lacking. There is absolute
silence upon everything south of Mexico. Guatemala
is known to have some very fine churches in remote
villages, designed to hold a much larger congregation
than the entire present population of these stranded settlements. It is possible to get some idea of them from
that delightful, pioneer work upon the Maya remains,
*Incidents of Travel in Central America, Chiapas, and Yuca-
tan*, by J. L. Stephens (London, 1841).

On the borders of Honduras and Guatemala, Stephens
passed seven gigantic churches in one day's march. The
best of them was at a village named Chiquimula; but none
of the seven that he saw was less than two hundred and
fifty feet long, and all had façades rich with sculpture and
carved statues larger than life. All these huge remains
were riven by earthquakes, and were as deserted, even in
his day, ninety years ago, as the Maya temples he had
come to visit. He, also, describes a celebrated pilgrimage church at Esquipulas. It stood on a stone platform,
a hundred and fifty feet broad, and had an immense
façade, a sculptured portal, and a nave with two aisles.
The pulpit was covered with gold leaf, and the altar had
a balustrade of silver pillars. The town of Guatemala,
itself, is uninteresting, for it was only founded in 1776.
Nevertheless, there are one or two fine palaces, chiefly

that of the Marqués Aycinena, the local grandee, and the situation of the town must be of incomparable beauty. Stephens describes the green valley that the city stands in, and the two huge volcanoes of Agua and Fuego that tower above it, one of them alive with fire, and the other dripping and overflowing with water. One is as dangerous as the other. Stephens beautifully describes the scenery, and the clusters of cocoanut trees that glittered in the sunbeams like plates of silver, at the feet of the two snow-clad volcanoes.

He, also, mentions Antigua, the old capital of Guatemala, so often destroyed by earthquakes and volcanic eruptions that it was practically deserted. The ruined cathedral was magnificent ; the grand altar stood under a cupola supported by sixteen great columns faced with tortoiseshell, and adorned with bronze medallions of exquisite workmanship. On the cornice there had been statutes of the Virgin and the Twelve Apostles in ivory. This cathedral was over three hundred feet long, and was lit by fifty windows. Near Antigua, the old town of Ciudad Vieja is equally rich in Spanish remains. Another old town, Quetzaltenango, has no less than seven great towering churches.

There must be remains of this sort in all the Central American republics. Stephens describes Leon, in Nicaragua, as full of buildings, and there are, doubtless, other places as interesting in San Salvador and in Costa Rica. The buildings begin, all over again, in a fresh outlet at Columbia. Here, again, there are old dead towns with great decaying churches and palaces.

After Mexico it might be expected that Peru would be the richest in this respect, and, if we add Ecuador, so as to form once again the old Empire of the Incas, this is certainly true of it. This gives us four centres, Arequipa, Lima, Cuzco, and Quito, and all four of them are full of Baroque buildings. Arequipa was the port of call for vessels from Manila and China. It was a wealthy town ; but nearly all its fine churches and houses were destroyed by the earthquake of 1868. Lima has a cathedral founded by Pizarro, and two immense convents, San Francisco and Santo Domingo. There are, also, two other fine churches with splendid Baroque façades – San Agustin and La Merced. The interiors of all these are characteristically rich. But Quito and Cuzco, the two Inca capitals, are of far greater interest. Cuzco has thirty churches and eleven convents. The cathedral and the church of the Jesuits stand in the same square, while there is another church, La Merced, with magnificent cloisters. The style of architecture is Cyclopean and monolothic, being formed largely from the remains of the old Inca buildings. The town must have swarmed, at one time, with monks and nuns ; both here and at Quito there is a great deal that deserves to be studied.

The Jesuit missionaries were busy in the hinterland of Peru, across the Andes, in the Montaña, and along the early reaches of the Amazon. Their activities were of a similar nature to what they accomplished in Paraguay, and, here again, the order was expelled in 1767, and everything they achieved has fallen into ruins. More especially did the Jesuits work along the head-waters of the Amazon, and the village of Laguna was among their chief settlements. The Carmelites, also, were active, and so were the Franciscans. Fine churches rose up, as if by magic, in these distant solitudes. The Jesuits owned enormous estates all over Peru, and even along its coast, the richest of them being San Xavier. It has a courtyard in the form of a stone cloister, with store-rooms and immense wine-presses on one side, and on the other is the handsome church. The carved woodwork of the pulpit and altars is magnificent, and the splendid gilt frames of the portraits of the generals of the order give the old church an air of grandeur.

Far away in the interior they built their churches and convents. These are in the same unvarying Baroque style, and the fact that for the first half of the seventeenth century the two kingdoms of Spain and Portugal were united under one head doubled the missionary energy of these two races, and sent their pioneers an immense distance into the centre of the continent. The Franciscans, as has been said, were only just behind the Jesuits, but they worked chiefly on the river Yucayali and its tributaries, leaving the Amazon to their rivals. They founded a big convent at a place called Ocopa; and, by 1740, they had no less than forty missions, which means that they had built that number of churches.

A most interesting book could be written on the subject of what the religious orders accomplished in the centre of South America. Nearly every traveller's book upon these regions makes some mention of the great ruined remains still left by them. Even a settlement so remote as Putumayo, the place of torture for the Indian rubber-gathering population, on a river which is one of the most distant tributaries of the Amazon, hundreds of miles inland over the snow-mountains from the Pacific, and literally some thousands of miles from the Atlantic, where the Amazon flows into it, has a Jesuit church of beautifully worked stone, the most elaborate internal carving, and a pharmacy and refectory, to the finishing of which many trained Indian artisans must have devoted their lifework.

Last of all, there is Brazil, about which a most irritating state of ignorance exists on the part of the Brazilians. Pernambuco, Para, Bahia, and Manaos, are literally full of churches, convents, and palaces. In the south of the country there are the States of Minas Geraes and São Paulo, containing cities like Ouro Preto, with its seven churches and many palaces, like Marianna, or like Cachoeira do Campo. This remote part of the world produced its legendary figures in the arts like Aleija-dinho, a cripple who had no hands and, working with tools strapped to his wrists, carved pulpits, confessionals, altar-screens, and statues, all over the State of Minas Geraes.

That a beautiful architecture existed in Brazil in the seventeenth and eighteenth centuries there is no shadow of doubt, but it is impossible to discover anything about it until someone who lives on the spot takes the trouble to investigate it. It is, of course, Portuguese in type ; a matter of brightly tinted walls, azulejos, Salomonic pillars, much gilding, and so forth. One day it will be written about, as will the history of the Jesuits in the wild wilderness of the Amazon. In the case of Brazil it will be of more particular interest, because that country would seem to have an assured future in the arts, and in music, now that Europe has destroyed itself in an idiot war, and that the Americans have pursued the wrong gods for too long and are beyond salvation. No country can afford to dispense with its own past, and least of all new countries peopled with the old European stock that produced all the wonders of our own decaying continent. May they realise this, too, before it is too late !

V

JESUIT SETTLEMENTS IN PARAGUAY

In conclusion, something must be said about the Jesuit settlements in Paraguay. They were the most southerly of all Spanish works, and, indeed, farther to the south of the world than any other works of Catholic activity. The Jesuits landed in this part of South America towards the end of the sixteenth century, and they marched far inland on their missionary enterprise till they came to the huge, rolling pampas plains of the interior. These districts were inhabited by the Guarani Indians, a race of naked savages, who, now that the Jesuits have left them, are back again, once more, in their primitive condition. The Jesuits set about the immediate conversion of these natives, and within twenty-five years of their first arrival in the country the Guaranis had altered their mode of life, and were living peaceably in the Misiones, or settlements designed for them by the Jesuits. These villages were uniformly alike in arrangement ; the church, with its monastery, was in the plaza, and the long tenement houses of the natives lay along the roads radiating from this centre. The houses were built on a fixed plan, and the Indians wore a costume which the Jesuits had designed for them. There were, altogether, thirty settlements of this description, eight of them being in the modern Paraguay, and the rest of them in Brazil, and in the Argentine provinces of Entre Rios, Corrientes, and Misiones.

This territory, which was ruled by the Jesuits like a
republic, lay far concealed, some one thousand or fifteen
hundred miles up country from the Gulf of La Plata.
The Guarani language was studied and written down,
and the Indians themselves taught to print books, or,
where this was impossible, to copy, with a pen, the
printed letters of a book in so close a fashion that the
forgery could not be told from the original. The great
missionary, Ruiz de la Montoya, who travelled for some
thirty years through the wilderness among the savage
Indians, was the author of the first book on the Guarani
language, while the Bible was soon after this translated
and printed in Guarani, and there is a book of sermons in
that language by the Indian Jesuit, Nicholas Yaparaguey.
These books, which are some of the most valuable of
bibliographical rarities, were printed and finished entirely
by the Indian workmen, and they bear the imprint of
the various settlements, principally that of the Misione
di S. Loreto.

The Indians were taught, also, every art connected
with the science of building ; they carved the statues
and painted the altar-pictures. Many of these churches
were of very great size, sometimes with as many as five
aisles, for the Jesuits were very rich from their cattle-
ranches and from the various objects that they exported,
on a fleet of their manufacture, down the La Plata river
to Montevideo and the great ports at its mouth. Maté,
the South American tea, coffee, and sugar, were part of
the sources of their wealth ; while some of the medicines
– as, for example, quinine – that they extracted from the
herbs and flowers of this region, were held in such value
that the Jesuits were directed to send every year a
quantity of their balsam of the Misiones for the use of the

pharmacy in the palace of Madrid. They supported an army of Indian troops, and on more than one occasion drove back the marauders, or Mamelukes, who had come eight hundred miles through the wilderness to attack them from the robber State of São Paulo de Piritinanga, the so-called Paulist republic, a colony of all the desperadoes who could reach it from every country.

The scene of this Jesuit paradise was of extreme beauty, hundreds of miles removed from snow-mountains or dangerous volcanoes ; and apparently so far away from human interference that war or pestilence did not enter into the calculations of those who built these colonies. There are huge rolling plains, with blue or red hills, far away, perhaps one hundred or one hundred and fifty miles into the distance ; and, to describe the flowers and trees with which they were familiar, I can only quote a paragraph from Mr. Cunninghame Graham, one of the few travellers who have visited this remote region. " The Croton Succirubrus (from which a resin known as the Sangre-de-drago is extracted), the Sumaha (bombax – the fruit of which yields a fine vegetable silk), the Ery-throxylon or coco of Paraguay, the Incienso or incense-tree of the Jesuits, are some of the most remarkable of the myriad shrubs. But if the shrubs are myriad, the flowers are past the power of man to count. Lianas, with their yellow and red and purple clusters of blossoms, like enormous bunches of grapes, hang from the forest trees. In the open glades upon the Trandubays, the Algarrotos, and the Espinillos, hang various orchidaceæ, called by the natives *flores de aire*, covering the trees with their aerial roots, their hanging blossoms, and their foliage of tender green. The Labiatæ, Compositæ, Daturæ, Umbelliferæ,

Convolvulaceæ, and many other species cover the ground in spring, or run up trees and bushes after the fashion of our honeysuckle, and traveller's joy."

Like all the aborigines of the American continent, the Indians had a very highly developed cult for these flowers, in connection with which they believed in many pagan traditions as to the origin or the different uses of each blossom. On particular feast-days they would decorate the whole interior of the church with flowers, and used to build up triumphal arches of them along the roads leading to the church door, while even the very trees by the roadside would be hung with flowers in such profusion that the branches seemed to be festooned with different coloured snows. The uniforms worn by the Indian notabilities on such occasions as this were of a gorgeous-ness in keeping with the colours of nature. "All the militia of the town " — I quote again from Mr. Cunning-hame Graham — " were in attendance, mounted upon their best horses, and armed with lances, bolas, lazos, and a few with guns. The officers of the Indians rode at their head, dressed out in gorgeous clothes, and troops of Indians, at stated intervals, performed a sort of pyrrhic dance between the squadrons of cavalry. In front of all, on a white horse, rode the Alferez Real, dressed in a doublet of blue velvet richly laced with gold, a waistcoat of brocade, and with short velvet breeches gartered with silver lace ; upon his feet, shoes decked with silver buckles, and the whole scheme completed by a gold-laced cocked hat. In his right hand he held the Royal Standard, fastened to a long cane which ended in a silver knob. Behind him came the Corregidor, arrayed in yellow satin, with a silk waistcoat and gold buttons, breeches of yellow velvet, and a magnificent hat. Other officials — the

GA

Commisario, the Maestro de Campo ; and the Sargente Major — were in scarlet coats, with crimson damask waistcoats trimmed with silver lace, red breeches, and black hats adorned with heavy lace."

It was their wealth and military strength which brought about the downfall and expulsion of the Jesuits, against whom charges of cruelty and extortion to the Indians were raised by their jealous neighbours. It is well established that these charges were unjustified ; but so great was their wealth at the time of their expulsion, in 1767, that in cattle alone their possessions reached the following figures : cattle, 719,761 ; horses, 27,204 ; sheep, 138,827 ; and oxen, 44,183. As soon as the Jesuits were removed (there were apparently only some four hundred of them among a population of as many hundred thousand Indians), the whole region fell back again into barbarism ; the churches and settlements were lost in the jungle, the Indians forgot everything they had been taught and became savages again, while so complete was the ruin that it is only within the last twenty years that settlements have sprung up once more in the neighbourhood of these towns, where the Jesuits once lived in peace among their Indian dependants for the space of a century and a half.

All of the Misiones are now a melancholy ruin, and the very stones of the buildings are covered under such a growth of tropical jungle that it is almost impossible to discover their whereabouts. There are a few carved stones, and one or two mutilated and broken statues, but, except for these, every sign of ornamental work has disappeared many years ago, for, after the expulsion of the order, every object of value was removed, and those that were too heavy were broken up and thrown out to rot away in the wet woods ; while the very natives, as I have said, relapsed again into barbarism, until, at this day, the Guarani Indians are among the most savage of the aborigines of South America.

VI

ABYSSINIA: GOA : AND THE SUMMER PALACE AT PEKIN

" GONDAR was, for a time, the capital of the old kingdom of Amhara, a part of Abyssinia. The Jesuit, Peter Paez, a Spaniard, arrived in the country in 1604. He was architect, mason, smith, and carpenter, and was able to manage with equal dexterity all the instruments used by each trade in the several stages of work. On the peninsula of Gorgora, a hilly, wooded promontory running about four miles into Lake Tana, he found a good quarry of white stone, and taught the workmen how to cut and lay the stones, using clay instead of mortar. At Gorgora, Paez built a church that was consecrated in 1621, and a magnificent palace for the Emperor ; on the plain of Dembea he built another very fine church, supported by Ionic columns, a bridge near Gondar, and another over the river Abbar, still standing. He probably rebuilt the famous church of Martolu Mariam, described by Dr. Beke.

" Dr. Beke discovered there an edifice, the walls of which were in a perfect state, built of stone in the form of a Roman cross. The interior was adorned with carvings of freestone of exquisite workmanship, as fresh and sharp as if recently executed.

" Many buildings were erected by workmen who had been formerly instructed by the Portuguese Jesuits, if not directly under their inspiration. For instance, the Emperor Fasilidas (1632–1665), who expelled the

Portuguese at the beginning of his reign, had a magnificent palace built by Indian masons and Abyssinian workmen containing an audience-hall one hundred and twenty feet long and surrounded by a stone wall thirty feet high and one and a half miles in circumference ; the palace was four stories high, flanked with towers, and defended by an inner and an outer battlemented wall.

" The same King also built, in 1645, the church of Takla Haymanot, the most celebrated of all the forty-four churches in and around Gondar, which was not destroyed until the Dervish invasion of 1857 ; and it was this monarch who really made Gondar a city, the capital of Abyssinia, and the centre of the trade of all that part of the country, with a population of 50,000. In spite of its magnificent situation, it has now been reduced by invasion and pillaging to a mere collection of huts clustered round these relics of bygone glory. The population is not more than 7,000 to 8,000."

These paragraphs are quoted from *In the Country of the Blue Nile*, by C. F. Rey, F.R.G.S. (Duckworth & Co., London, 1927). There is no doubt that Gondar was a Portuguese Baroque town of the early seventeenth century, and its ruins should be, even now, of distinct architectural interest.

Their activities in Africa were not confined to that. Portuguese East Africa and Portuguese West Africa have the towns of Mozambique, Angola, and São Paulo de Loanda. Mozambique has belonged to Portugal since 1507, and Angola since 1575. The religious orders were as busy as usual, and have left plenty of evidence of their activity in the way of ruined churches and monasteries.

The capital of the Portuguese Empire in India was Goa. It had, at one time, a population of some 200,000, but it fell into decadence, and, in 1790, the Viceroy removed from it to New Goa, five miles away. In 1890 there were only eighty-six fever-haunted inhabitants living in the old capital.

It has four or five churches of great splendour. The Church of Bom Jesus, built in 1594, contains the body of St. Francis Xavier, and is the principal building of the place. Its high and complicated façade runs straight on into that of another huge building with lofty halls and immense corridors, the Convent of the Jesuits, which was finished in 1590, some forty years after the death of St. Francis. This was the college from which so many missionaries were sent forth to India, China, and Japan ; but the Jesuits were expelled by Pombal in 1759, and their property confiscated by the Government. Before that, the town swarmed with monks and nuns ; about the year 1700, Goa is said to have contained as many as 30,000 of them. By 1835, all the monastic orders had been driven out ; but the endowments of the churches have never been forfeited, and so the archbishop and the secular clergy of Goa still receive large allowances from the Portuguese Republic.

The Church of Bom Jesus is entered by a side-door from the Jesuits' college, through the sacristy, a huge room with wardrobes filled with embroidered vestments. The tomb and shrine of St. Francis Xavier occupy a side-chapel. His monument consists of three tiers of sarcophagi made of jasper and marble, and given, in the year 1696, by the Grand Duke Cosmo III of Tuscany. The upper tier is decorated with inlaid panels in Florentine mosaic, representing scenes in the life of the saint, and on the top of this is his body in an enormous silver coffin ; while on the altar is a life-size statue in solid silver given by Queen Maria of Portugal late in the eighteenth century.

A little distance away is the Sé Primacial, or Cathedral of St. Catherine, built between 1562 and 1623, which still has a staff of twenty-eight canons, who live in the archbishop's palace, a magnificent building next door ; the archbishop, who is Patriarch of the Indies, on occasion resides here, while the Viceroy, on his periodical visits, stops in the neighbouring monastery. In front of the cathedral the Palace of the Inquisition used to stand; and it was in this square that the terrible autos-da-fé were held, at which, so typical of religious controversy, the Nestorians, the primitive Christians of India, suffered much more than the Hindus. At the other corner of this huge square were the buildings of the Misericordia which enclosed the Church of Nossa Senhora da Serra, built by Albuquerque in fulfilment of a vow, and in which he was originally buried. The Palace of the Viceroys is nearly in ruins, but it still shows traces of its once famous windows, in which the panes were made, not of glass, but out of sheets of mother-of-pearl. Beyond this there lie the Great Bazaar, the vast domed and double-towered Church of San Cajetano, the convents of the Dominicans and Carmelites, and the renowned missionary college of St. Paul, or Santa Fé.

To conclude these evidences of Portuguese activities in this direction we may pass by Ceylon, which contains, nevertheless, the ruins of several churches built by them, and must devote a paragraph to the description of Macao. They settled in this region, just opposite Hong-Kong, about 1560. It has arcaded streets of blue or rose-coloured houses, crumbling terraces walled with cracked tiles, and deserted streets with grass growing in them. There are at least three Baroque churches : the cathedral, São Lorenzo, and São Paulo. This last is in ruins, but a great stone staircase leads to it, and the gateway, like a triumphal arch, is still intact. It was burnt down, a century ago, by Chinese fanatics. The monastery and the interior of the church were completely destroyed, but the granite façade of the church still stands. There are three doorways with Ionic pillars, and, above, five niches framed in by Corinthian pillars. The great gateway, already mentioned, remains to show how Oriental was the character of this building, and it was, indeed, the work of workmen imported by the Jesuits from Japan.

Macao must be a most picturesque ruin, with its deserted, grass-grown streets, its gambling-dens, its memories of Camoëns. It is, also, of interest as a small sample of what might have happened, and it was no impossibility, had the Daimyō Nobunaga lived and the Jesuits been able, through his influence and favour, to Christianise Japan. Then, there would have been extraordinary developments, but whether the results of it would have been in questionable taste, or not, there is luckily no reason to discuss. Certainly the Jesuits would have found themselves in the position of engine-drivers to a very formidable and energetic force. For at least a century they had their eyes upon the possibility of it; at one moment there were said to be half a million native converts, and at any rate we have sufficient knowledge of what the Jesuits accomplished in other countries to be sure of the impetus it would have given to architecture and the minor arts.

The mention of these dead possibilities gives an

opportunity, now we are so near the scene of it, to devote
a few lines to the Summer Palace of the Chinese
Emperors, near Pekin, for this, also, was a work of the
Jesuits. The group of pavilions that formed the Summer
Palace was built during three reigns, K'ang-hsi, Yung-
ch'eng, and Ch'ien-lung. This latter Emperor united the
different palaces. In 1737 he entrusted the general plan
of the European pavilions in it to Fra Castiglione, and
ten years later he made Père Benôist his architect.

The Jesuit Attiret, who was painter to Ch'ien-lung,
writes as follows, in 1743 : " Hillocks from twenty to
sixty feet high have been thrown up, forming an endless
number of little valleys. Canals of clear water, coming
from the high mountains which dominate the country,
water these valleys, and, after dividing, re-unite to form
fountains, lakes, and seas.

" The slopes of the hills and mounds are covered with
the flowering-trees so common in China. The canals
have no alignment ; the rustic stonework which borders
them is arranged with so much art that one might take it
for Nature's own handiwork. Here the canal widens,
there it narrows ; its banks are gay with flowers growing
in the rocks, and each season brings fresh variety and adds
its peculiar charm.

" From one of the valleys the buildings can be seen.
The whole façade seems to be nothing but windows
and columns ; the woodwork is gilded, painted, and
lacquered ; the walls are of grey brick, well shaped and
well glazed. The roofs are covered with glazed tiles, red,
yellow, blue, and violet, which, by their combination and
arrangement, make a pleasing variety of compartments
and designs.

" Each valley has its pavilion, small, considering the

extent of the whole enclosure, but large enough to accommodate the greatest of our lords with his suite. Several of these pavilions are built with cedarwood, which is brought from 500 li away, and, in this vast enclosure, more than two hundred such palaces may be counted, without reckoning the pavilions of the eunuchs.

" The canals are crossed by bridges of very varied form. The balustrades of some are of white marble, well worked and sculptured in bas-relief. In the middle of the large lake rises, on a rock, a little palace with a central point that the architect chose as giving the finest view of the whole park. The larger lakes are crossed in magnificent boats, and some of these are big enough to take the place of a fine, large house.

" In the Emperor's apartments can be seen the most beautiful things imaginable in furniture, ornaments, paintings in the Chinese taste, antique vases, porcelains, gold and silver cloths, and silks. Everything that art and good taste can add to the wealth of Nature has been brought together here. Of all the Europeans about the place, only the painters and the clock-makers have, as their work necessitates, access to all parts."

The Jesuit Benôist was in charge of the hydraulic works, and cast for the Emperor a fountain which served as water-clock, whose twelve animals cast jets, in turn, during two hours each. Finally, the waters of a river were harnessed and led into a large reservoir to feed the fountains and cascades.

The palace, which we must regard, not as a chinoiserie, but its opposite, a phantasy upon European taste, was destroyed by the English during the war of 1860. The French were the first of the allied forces to enter the

Summer Palace after the Emperor had fled, in the night, to Jehol. The French officers visited all the fourteen palaces, but ordered that nothing should be touched till the English arrived. Then, by the orders of Lord Elgin, the palace was looted and set on fire, a measure with which the French general refused to associate himself.

A few more details of the Summer Palace may be quoted from a traveller who visited the ruins some twenty years later. "We came across a stone roadway running round the lake, then an immense marble bridge with seventeen arches, leading to an artificial island. It was covered with rockwork in which grottoes and caves had been constructed, and was big enough to contain several important buildings, such as guards' quarters, pagodas, and a pavilion for the Emperor. A little to the right of the island may be seen the 'hunchback' bridge, entirely of marble, which is only accessible by foot because of its acute angle. Near it is an island like a little fortress, surrounded by crenellated walls and overhung by the roofs and masts of pagodas. Still on the edge of the lake, there is a marble junk lying a yard or two from the shore. Near it is an elegant pavilion built on a bridge, with two marble pillars carrying lions. The hill is climbed by immense flights of steps, at the head of each of which is a landing. Halfway up is a bronze temple, every piece of which was cast by the Jesuits. Its base is of white marble. Finally, the height is crowned by a vast structure, in style half Hindu, half Western. Its walls are of yellow enamelled bricks, and it is covered with little niches varnished green. In each of these is a yellow porcelain idol. A few steps away is an immense portico with a wonderful panorama stretching before it."

This catalogue of strange effects reads like Hogarth's

notes to his illustrations of wrong perspective. Everything is just upside down and where it ought not to be. It is very difficult to arrive at the truth about the Summer Palace, although there are prints of some parts of it, made by Chinese artists under the direction of the Jesuit fathers. Some idea of the skill of their pupils can be got from the astronomical instruments taken from Pekin in 1900 and now at Potsdam. The destruction of the Summer Palace must always be a matter for regret. The name of the person who gave the order for this act of vandalism is the same as that of the spoliator of the Parthenon. Perhaps he may have been present, in the spirit, at Delhi, after the Indian Mutiny, when the English turned the Moghul Palace, perhaps the most magnificent palace that has ever been erected, into a cavalry barracks.

BIBLIOGRAPHY

This is a list of the few old books that may be useful. No alphabetical or chronological order is attempted.

Fra Francisco de los Santos : *Descripcion breve del Monasterio di S. Lorenzo del Escorial.* Madrid, 1657.
(A panegyric – if ever there was one – in Gongoristic prose ; but it was written before Luca Giordano's visit to Spain and it has, therefore, no mention of his frescoes on the vaults of the church, or on the ceiling of the great staircase. An English translation was published in 1760.)

Fra João di São Joseph do Prado : *Monumento Sacro di Mafra.* Lisboa, 1751.

Fra Manoel dos Santos : *Alcobaça Illustrada.* Coimbra, 1710.

Don Juan de Vera Tassis y Villaroel : *Noticias de la Enfermedad de Donna Maria Luisa de Borbon.* Madrid, 1690.
(With a plate of the Queen's catafalque designed by Churriguerra and engraved by Ruiz de la Iglesia.)

Francisco Xavier de Casteneda : *Il Transparente.* Toledo, 1732.
(An epic poem addressed to the Churriguerresque "Transparente" in the Cathedral of Toledo.)

P.M. Fr. Enrique Florez : *Espana Sagrada.* Madrid, 1750.

La Torre Farfan : *Fiestas de Sevilla.* Seville, 1672.
(This book has several fine engravings by Valdes Leál (1622–1690), a native of Cordoba, and one of the best painters of the School of Seville.)

Padre Pedro Lozano : *La Descripcion geografica del Gran Chaco.* Cordoba, 1733.
(One of the few contemporary Spanish authorities on Jesuit Paraguay.)

William Bullock : *Six Months' Residence in Mexico.* London, 1824.
(Illustrated with sixteen splendid aquatints, four of which are in colours.)

H. G. Ward : *Mexico in 1827.* London, 1828.
(Illustrated with twenty-one aquatints, eighteen of them in colour.)

MODERN AUTHORITIES

Biblioteca de Autores Españoles, vol. xlvi. Madrid, 1858.
(The funeral discourse on the architect Ventura Rodriguez, by Jovellanos, here reprinted, contains most interesting comments on the Churriguerresque architecture that Rodriguez succeeded in expelling from Spain.)

Otto Schubert : *Geschichte des Barock en Spanien.* Paul Neff Verlag. Esslingen, 1908.

August L. Mayer : *Alt-Spanien.* Delphin Verlag. Munich, 1921.

Constantin Uhde : *Baudenkmaler in Spanien und Portugal.* Ernst Wasmuth Verlag. Berlin.

François Rousseau : *Règne de Charles III d'Espagne.*

André Michel : *Histoire de l'Art,* vol. iv., part ii., pp. 855–869.
(For illustrations of the Manoeline buildings in Portugal.)

W. Lübke and M. Semrau : *Der Kunst der Barockzeit.* Stuttgart, 1905.

A. Danvila Jaldero : *La Archittettura Churriguerresqua in Historia y Arte.* Madrid, April 1896.
(Contains interesting information about the architects in question.)

J. F. Rafols : *Arquitectura del Renacimiento Espanol.* Barcelona, 1929.
(A most excellent handbook.)

Danvers : *The Portuguese Empire in India : its Rise and Decline.*

José N. da Fonseca : *An Historical Sketch of the City of Goa.* Bombay, 1878.

C. A. Montalto de Jesus : *Historic Macao.* Hong-Kong, 1902.

R. B. Cunninghame Graham : *A Vanished Arcadia – the Jesuits in Paraguay, 1607–1767.* London, 1901.
(The best authority on this subject.)

W. H. Koebel : *In Jesuit Land.* London, 1912.
(With an introduction by R. B. Cunninghame Graham.)

Arte e Natureza em Portugal : 8 vols., 1901–1908.

William Beckford : *Sketches of Spain and Portugal.* 1834.

Marcel Dieulafoy : *Espagne et Portugal.* Paris, 1903.

Count Raczynski : *Les Arts en Portugal.* 1846.
Dictionnaire Historico-Artistique de Portugal. 1847.

C. Crum Watson : *Portuguese Architecture.* London, 1908.

Martin Hume : *Through Portugal.* London, 1907.

Guia de Portugal : Edited by the National Library of Lisbon, in 2 vols., 1924 and 1928.

Albrecht Haupt : *Die Baukunst der Renaissance in Portugal.* 1890–1895.

Léon Poinsard : *Le Portugal Inconnu.* Paris, 1910.

A Arte em Portugal.
(A most useful series of monographs published by Marqués Abreu, Oporto, 1928–1930. Nine volumes have already appeared, including Oporto, Braga, Vila do Conde, Viana do Costelo Evora, and Mafra. Others are promised for Guimaraes, Aveiro, Lamego, Vizeu, Guarda, etc., etc.)

Portugal : *Les Guides Blues.* Paris, 1931.
(A completely new, excellent, and indispensable guide to the country.)

Walter H. Kilham : *Mexican Architecture of the Vice-regal Period.* London, 1927.

Manuel G. Revilla : *El Arte en Mejico.* Mejico, 1893.

The Architectural Record, vol. xxxvii. January to June, 1915.
(Articles on Mexican architecture.)

F. Sylvester Baxter : *Spanish Colonial Architecture.* Boston, U.S.A., 1901.
(This is the pioneer authority upon the subject.)

T. P. Terry : *Terry's Guide to Mexico.* Ed. 1923.
(Excellent and comprehensive, with special notes on Mexican architecture.)

Genaro Garcia and Antonio Cortes : *La Architectura en Mexico.* Museo Nacional de Archæologia. Mejico, 1914.
(Contains fine photographs of Mexican churches.)

F. Dies Barroso : *El Arte en la Nueva Espana.* Compania de Artes Graficas. Mejico, 1922.

Madame Calderon de la Barca : *Life in Mexico.*
(This is one of the most delightful travel diaries in existence. It was first published, with a preface by Prescott, the historian, in 1843. It has been reprinted in the Everyman Library, but is now, once more, out of print.)

Various monographs published by the Ministry of Education for Mexico, from 1925 onwards. Their author is Dr. Atl. They have delightful coloured illustrations, which give some idea of the extraordinary colour-schemes of Mexican architecture, and their notes are most valuable. Five volumes have so far been